R E L E A S E

RELEASE

CREATE A CLUTTER FREE AND SOUL DRIVEN LIFE

Peggy Fitzsimmons, Ph.D

Waterside Productions

Waterside Productions

2055 Oxford Ave
Cardiff, CA 92007
www.waterside.com

TABLE OF CONTENTS

INTRODUCTION

Whenever I tell someone that I declutter for a living, they invariably say "Ohhh! I need that!" Then they pull me aside for a quick consult about the closet full of clothes they never wear, the stuff their grandma left them they don't really want, and the never-ending piles of paper in their office. They tell me life is "crazy busy" and that their house is in perpetual chaos. They share how they feel chronically anxious and how they take the edge off with a nightly glass, or two or three, of wine. Pretty soon they're talking about their relationship troubles, and something that happened a few years ago that still keeps them up at night, and how they hate their job but could never make a living doing what they really want to do.

At some point, they wistfully say how great it would be to get rid of everything— including their family—and move to a small cottage at the beach with their dog. And then they drop to a whisper and reveal their deeper secret: "I just don't feel connected to anything, you know...spiritual." I feel their longing to release the clutter in their lives and come home to themselves. Sometimes they reach out to me to help them get started. Very often they don't, but I know they want to. Their soul is calling to them, but they aren't sure they can heed the call. Since you picked up this book, you're also hearing the call. Don't worry. You're not going crazy. You're just waking up.

We all live with clutter. Most of us are buried in stuff that isn't essential to our lives and definitely isn't in alignment with who we are spiritually. Physical clutter is the most obvious, but we're also burdened by mental, emotional, energetic, and relationship clutter. Hoarding has become a dirty word, but it simply means amassing things for preservation or future use. This is what we do. We accumulate inner and outer things that we think serve us, and we hold on for dear life. I hate to break the news to you, but we're all hoarders.

Hoarding is like taking a deep breath, then holding it, and holding it, and holding it, refusing to exhale. If we won't let go, we stop the natural flow of taking in what we need right now and releasing what we don't. If we won't let go, we can't share our resources with those that need them—think of the plants that depend on our exhale for life-giving carbon dioxide. And if we won't let go, we can't make space for new breath.

Everything we hold onto carries weight. It might be mental weight, like the weight of jealous thoughts; or physical weight, like the weight of the old set of encyclopedias in the basement; or emotional weight, like the weight of conflict with a family member. Everything we hold onto has a cost. It might be an emotional cost, like the cost of spending too much time in sadness; an energetic cost, like the cost of keeping up with society's ever-speeding treadmill; a relationship cost, like the cost of not accepting someone's choice for a partner; or a financial cost, like the cost of having to wash the car every week because it doesn't fit in the jam-packed garage.

And everything we hold onto requires energy from us. It might be mental energy, like the amount it takes to stay prepared for the next bad thing that is sure to happen; or emotional energy, like the kind it takes to feel angry all the time; or physical energy, like the effort it takes to keep all the tchotchkes on the bookshelf dust-free. Everything we hold onto that doesn't serve us ultimately leaves us drained and overwhelmed, restlessly seeking something spiritual that is already present within us, though obscured by our clutter.

I have my ex-husband Ralph to thank for putting me on the road of decluttering. He didn't have many possessions but took care of the ones he had. We lived with what we needed and little extra. The open space and simple furnishings of our home were clean, beautiful, enough. Although we didn't have a lot of physical clutter, all kinds of other clutter lived in our house. The mental and emotional clutter of fear and insecurity were ever-present. The energy of mistrust and striving clogged the air. The relationship clutter of fixing and controlling took up more space than accepting and supporting. Still, underneath all that clutter was a deep love and many moments of harmony. I never understood why we couldn't sustain those moments. Now I know we were moving in and out of our "right minds," inconsistently letting go and making room for the truth of our souls.

I spent the years after my divorce diving deep into my clutter. I uncovered lots of stuff I had been holding onto that wasn't really me. For example, I carried around boxes of secrets and shame from having been molested by a neighbor as a child, convinced they belonged to me. I walked through life wearing un-safety glasses, seeing people as potential enemies out to harm me. I spent a lot of time feeling sad, lonely, and afraid. I couldn't find my center in the midst of other people's energy. I trusted other people's opinions more than my own knowing.

I believed I wasn't good enough and tried to assuage that feeling by achieving all the way to a Ph.D. I presided over my own private courtroom, judge and jury of myself and everyone else. And I did lots of things that weren't true to my soul, like wasting precious time on stuff that didn't matter; getting caught up in the drama of the day; consuming crappy food, Parliaments, and lots of Diet Coke; buying stuff to fill voids that couldn't be filled with material things; competing for approval and validation; hurting other people; violating boundaries by trying to be everyone's healer, and allowing my own boundaries to be violated in hopes of getting a nugget of love. Deep down, I knew there was another way. I had been given glimpses. Clear and beautiful glimpses of my soul and the souls of others, where I felt only love, acceptance, joy, peace, connection, harmony, and freedom. I knew that was the truth, and the rest was a lie. So I stayed committed to finding out: Who am I truly? Who are you truly? And where can we meet that's true?

It's been a good road to travel, despite getting lost many times, running into detours, running out of gas, and occasionally crashing and burning. The best part of the trip has been realizing there's always another crossroad ahead; a stop sign at the corner of stuff and soul where I can choose to pause, turn in the direction of who I really am, and share my love, rather than my clutter, with the world.

While on my own journey, I've had the honor of companioning many people on their roads to decluttering. The more I did the work, the more I felt compelled to say, "Stop the insanity!" The insanity of fear, greed, unworthiness, stress, and never enough. The insanity of forgetting who we are and what we're here for. The insanity of house upon house, in town after town, from one city to the next filled with stuff, yet the people living in them still feeling lack and spiritually bereft.

So I decided to write this book. I knew it could provide good company for anyone hearing the call and would keep me purposefully on my soul road. I knew it would allow me to share, rather than hoard, the teachings and experiences I've had. If I could tell you the layers of clutter that revealed themselves in the process. Oy! But staying with it strengthened my conviction about the truth of clutter and the truth of the soul. I did my best to cut to the essentials and make this book meaning-full and clutter-free. My goal is to offer support to help you answer the question: *my stuff or my soul?* and to provide practical tools for your journey. Everything in these pages is something I've encountered in myself or with clients. Everything in these pages is something I've learned, am still learning, and forgot five minutes ago but might remember tomorrow. Stay light as you read, play with the information, and see what miracles happen on the road ahead. It'll be fun. Promise.

ONE

THE JOURNEY OF RELEASING: FROM CLUTTER TO FREEDOM

Being alive requires of us a relationship with the
mysterious, lifelong experience of letting go.
—*Molly Fumia*

The Divine and Human Aspects Within Us

My take on decluttering is unapologetically spiritual. I believe there is a spirit embodied in all of us, which I will call the soul. Think of the soul as our essence, our higher self, our true nature. It's the aspect of us that is expansive, eternal, and inherently wise and loving. It holds our highest intelligence about what's right and true. It knows peace and abundance, and experiences joy, wonder, passion, and gratitude. It is free and unattached, yet deeply connected to everyone and everything. The soul is the **divine** in us. We are all souls inhabiting human bodies, hanging out together here on planet Earth for a while. More than just humans, we are human *beings* infused with spirit. We are in this world but not of it. We're here on a journey to realize who we are and allow our souls to be in the driver's seat of our lives.

Yet, we all have another aspect that fights for the wheel, called the ego. Think of the ego as our psyche, our personality, our sense of self. It's the image we construct of ourselves; the beliefs, needs, roles, and possessions we identify with and show to the world. The ego is concerned with self-preservation. It competes for everything to ensure our safety, success, and survival. It knows conflict and lack, and experiences fear, insecurity, loneliness, and anger. It sees us as separate from all other beings and even from the earth itself. The ego is the **human** aspect of us. It's the false self that we mistake for our true self, and it is the driver of our lives more than we know.

The *being* consciousness of our soul and the *human* consciousness of our ego engage with life **very** differently. Take some time with the following examples to feel into these two aspects within yourself:

The soul lives in love; the ego lives in fear. The soul accepts; the ego judges. The soul trusts; the ego doubts. The soul is at peace; the ego is in conflict. The soul knows it's never alone; the ego is desperate to belong. The soul knows it's worthy and necessary; the ego seeks validation. The soul extends love; the ego withholds love. The soul is content; the ego is dissatisfied. The soul takes life as it comes; the ego controls. The soul is harmonious; the ego needs to be right. The soul cooperates; the ego competes. The soul knows nothing is permanent; the ego fears change. The soul surrenders; the ego forces. The soul shares; the ego acquires. The soul knows everything is connected; the ego feels separate. The soul is eternal; the ego fears death. The soul lets go; the ego holds on.

Essentially, we are of two minds, shifting endlessly between them. This is the human condition. But knowing who's at the wheel at any given moment matters, because **which mind** we come from determines our thoughts and emotions, the energy we exude, the way we relate to others, and the actions we take. If we identify primarily with our ego mind, our lives become clutterfull. Here's why. When the ego is in the driver's seat, the song on the radio is "Not Enough." It goes like this: *I am not enough, you are not enough, and there is not enough.* This is how the ego experiences the world. It puts forth thoughts rooted in scarcity, separation, and survival which in turn create emotions such as anxiety, fear, shame, and frustration. These emotions carry low vibration energies, like needing, wanting, striving, and resisting. With the ego at the wheel, our relationships are characterized by judging, competing, fixing, and loving conditionally. And our homes become warehouses for more stuff than we know what to do with, yet we keep acquiring more.

Put simply, the ego drives us to accumulate all kinds of inner and outer clutter. If we don't believe we are enough, we chronically feel unworthy and unsuccessful by society's measure. If we don't believe others are enough, we're never quite sure we are safe, can depend on others, or find our tribe. If we don't think there is enough, we fear we won't have what we need or will lose whatever we do have. The not enough of the ego mind creates fear and suffering. And our clutter is this fear and suffering made visible.

For example, with the ego as navigator of our lives, we stockpile resentments in our minds; feel stressed more often than not; seek approval and validation at every turn; or hang onto relationships that bring us pain. We love ourselves only when we fit in our jeans; relentlessly judge other people's choices; need to have the last word; or run ourselves ragged trying to keep up with the Joneses. We consume bad food and designer bags, fill our houses to the brim with things we don't even use, and rely on other people to fill the emptiness we feel inside. We even ignore our impact on the earth to get what we think we need. Because the ego is obsessed with self-preservation, it clings to everything that isn't really us; our pride, our looks, our wealthy but cheating partners, our status as CEO, our shame at not being CEO, our opinions, our youth, our stories, our rage, our mistakes, our rusty tools, our old recipe books. In ego consciousness, letting go feels like certain death.

Meanwhile, our souls wait patiently for us to wake up and recognize our true nature; to *self-realize*. If we identify primarily with our soul mind, our lives become clutter-free. Here's how it works. When the soul is in the driver's seat, the song on the radio is "Enough is Enough." It goes like this: *I am enough, you are enough, and there is enough.* This is how the soul experiences the world. It puts forth thoughts of abundance, connection, and safety which in turn lead to emotions such as gratitude, joy, and appreciation. These emotions carry high vibration energies like expansiveness, peace, and acceptance. With the soul at the wheel, our relationships are characterized by harmony, collaboration, and sharing love. And our homes contain the things we really love and truly need. The soul drives us to live with only the inner and outer things that affirm who we really are.

If we believe we are enough, we feel worthy, secure, and successful by our own measure. If we believe others are enough, we trust we are safe, can depend on others, and are already in our tribe. If we believe there is enough, we know we always have what we need and can share freely. Living from the enough of our soul mind moves us out of suffering and into freedom, to a place where clutter can't exist.

Our soul's freedom is visible when we naturally think kind thoughts about ourselves and others; appreciate what we have; trust our decisions; and feel prosperous no matter our checking account balance. It's present when we put forth positive energy in the world; feel content; inspire someone else to succeed; love ourselves no matter what; and share our possessions. The soul is free of fear. It doesn't cling to anything. Why would it? It's eternal and ever-connected. It knows we're more than our self-judging thoughts, the mood we're in, the illness we're facing, the clothes we wear, the car we drive, and our fear that there isn't enough. It knows we are here for one purpose; to share our love with the world in our unique ways. In soul consciousness, letting go feels like the best and only thing to do.

Dead Ends and Open Roads

As we travel through life, our ego mind tends to get the most drive time. We're individually hypnotized by the ego, and collectively entranced in a like-minded society that celebrates and rewards the false self while ignoring and devaluing the soul. We find ourselves in mental and emotional turmoil, obsessed with our individual needs, addicted to material comforts, consumed by mindless consuming, disconnected from nature, squared off in constant competition, and walking with fear as our most loyal companion. Taking the trip with the ego at the wheel leads to dead end after dead end. But what to do? We have to turn to the soul.

The root cause of clutter is *misidentifying* ourselves. To release clutter, we have to inhabit the truth that we are human beings, here to know ourselves as we are and put our love into action. As we broaden our definition of ourselves to include our spiritual identity, we recognize that the habitual thoughts, emotions, energies, and actions of the ego mind are only one aspect of us, not all of us.

We realize that just by being here on this planet, we are necessary and worthy. We know our unique light is needed to illuminate the world. We remember we are all spiritual beings, all connected, and, at our core, the same. We understand we live in a global village, inherently interdependent on each other and the earth itself. With our souls at the wheel and our egos riding shot-gun, we find ourselves on the open road, wind in our hair, and much less traffic.

When you picked up this book, you were hearing the call to head out on a new road. To leave the prison of who you are not for the freedom of who you are. To fall out of step with the herd of egos and into step with the truth of your soul. Take a moment right now to imagine yourself as a decluttered soul; an agent of love, rather than fear, moving in the world with light energy and a minimal footprint. Focusing on what really matters. Relying on your inner knowing. Allowing things to come and go. Inhabiting a home and office environment worthy of who you are. Engaging responsibly with other people. And being living permission for others to say "enough already."

If you can visualize a world full of decluttered souls, sharing their love and unique gifts, you'll never have to wonder if the trip is worth taking. In fact, restoring the soul in ourselves and our world is the ONLY trip worth taking.

Love Your Ego Mind

Now let's be very clear. The ego is not a bad thing. We don't have to push it out of the car and speed off in a cloud of dust. In fact, we can't. The ego is forever a part of our human existence. But giving it license to drive keeps our attention and energy focused on our false selves and the false selves of others.

The ego deserves respect. It has a very big job after all. It creates, maintains, and protects our sense of self. Its job description reads: *must keep human safe, secure, successful, and surviving.* To do its job, the ego holds onto what is familiar, and therefore comfortable. Now being buried in clutter is not one bit comfortable. It is, however, familiar. And there is comfort in what's familiar, no matter how uncomfortable it is. Our ego is convinced we need all our stuff to keep us safe, validate our (ahem, false) selves, and be prepared for anything life might throw at us. It does its best to keep us right where we are.

That's why the key to decluttering is to love your ego mind. Say what? Stay with me here. To release clutter, you have to treat your ego with compassion. You have to know it for what it is and appreciate it for what it's trying to do. Remember, the ego operates from fear. For people who struggle with clutter, this fear is closer to terror. The ego resists change, because change is a threat to its survival. From the ego's perspective, if it doesn't survive, we don't either. Because of this, it puts up strong resistance to our soul becoming the navigator of our lives. It constantly grabs for the wheel to establish itself as the mind in the driver's seat. Our job is to honor and soothe this fear (or terror) by loving our ego enough to move slowly. When we do, it quiets down and moves over to the passenger seat. And our soul can slide behind the wheel, buckle the ego's seatbelt, and head off on new roads.

Once the ego is in its well-deserved seat as copilot, we can employ it in service to our soul. We can enlist its skills of creating, maintaining, and protecting our true self rather than our false self. We can gently introduce it to things of our true nature, so it can work on our behalf to make them our new personal reality. This is what the ego does after all; it brings our life into alignment with how we see ourselves. It affirms whomever we declare ourselves to be. If we offer it thoughts like *I am safe*, emotions like gratitude, energies like enthusiasm, ways of relating like acceptance, or less stuff—and our world doesn't fall apart—it becomes comfortable and familiar with a new sense of being.

Here is a simple practice to give your ego mind new things to relate to and prime it for decluttering. Take some time today to notice things that represent the truth of your soul. For example, when you see a person out exercising, acknowledge their vitality and the vitality that lives in you. As you walk by a flowering tree, feel into its beauty and the beauty within you. When you hear someone give a compliment, acknowledge their generosity and the generosity inside you. If you witness a kind exchange in the coffee shop, sense that harmony and the harmony that lives in you. When you see someone give something of value away, acknowledge their abundance and the abundance within you.

This practice interrupts our ego's usual approach to life and gives it a safe way to experience things of the soul. Every new experience that doesn't lead to our demise helps the ego relax into a new sense of self. With the ego gainfully employed as copilot, our souls are free to take the wheel and get our houses in order.

The Truth About Clutter

Decluttering is an invitation to look at everything in our lives to determine if it is essential. If it is *of our essence*. Anything that isn't in alignment with our true nature of peace, acceptance, generosity, vitality, harmony, and love is clutter. We can have clutter in our inner environment—untrue thoughts, negative emotions, outdated belief systems, or low vibration energies—or in our outer environments—relationships that aren't nourishing, ways of relating that affirm our false selves, habits that diminish our energy and health, and endless possessions. Regardless, all forms of clutter are equal. A stuffed drawer, a relationship secret, a frantic energy, a pattern of feeling lonely, a belief you are less than, a nightly ice cream binge, a trash can in the laundry room overflowing with lint, a trash can in your heart overflowing with guilt, or a dirty shelf piled high with mismatched tupperware all reflect the same thing; **a soul not being true to itself.**

Treating clutter this way keeps our eyes fixed clearly on the road. It also puts us in position to connect the dots between the different forms of clutter. Here's an example.

> *A few years ago, I worked with Julie. Her house was pristine and quite literally took my breath away. White walls, white furniture, white rugs. Sacred objects everywhere: crystals and candles and bells and singing bowls, each carefully placed and beautifully spaced. It was like a soul's delight meditation center. Then I opened the bedroom closet. Whoa, it was a different story in there! It was literally jammed floor to ceiling, stuff balanced precariously on top of more stuff. Now that was curious. So I invited her to get curious .... what was this space communicating? Julie began to reveal how her relationship life was out of integrity. She was a yoga and meditation teacher, practicing the art of soul consciousness, but she was involved sexually with several different men, including one who was married. The physical clutter in her bedroom closet revealed the relationship clutter she was hiding behind closed doors.*

Our inner and outer spaces tend to reflect each other this way. The good news is that dealing with one area of clutter automatically impacts another. Any action we take elegantly shifts something else, because all forms of clutter reflect the same thing—a soul not being true to itself—and are thus connected. In Julie's example, clearing the clutter in the bedroom closet would have some kind of impact on her relationship clutter, and clearing the clutter in her relationships would have some kind of impact on the physical clutter in the closet. What that impact will be is unknown. That's the fun part. That's the journey.

To free ourselves, we have to be willing to look at all the different forms of clutter in our lives because they're all connected. So stay curious. For example, what does your pajama drawer really say about you? How does a moment of fear affect the energy you bring to a conversation? What does having your own melt down during your child's temper tantrum reflect about your thinking? How does holding onto the wedding dress from your first marriage serve you? How do you really feel when you criticize your wife? If you are willing to follow the breadcrumbs of connection, they will lead you home to your true nature.

The (Unpopular) Truth About Decluttering

Freeing ourselves from clutter is a lifelong journey. There, I said it. Most people don't want to hear that. They think decluttering is about getting rid of their stuff all at once, and once and for all. Sometimes it seems possible, like in those TV shows where they come in with trucks and hazmat suits and throw everything away, leaving the hoarder happily sipping tea in her new kitchen. In my experience, that's not how it really goes. Staying in touch with the truth of our soul, and acting from it, is an ongoing process. It requires us to hold the vision of a soul-driven life and stay aware of who is occupying the driver's seat at any given moment. But don't despair! Rather than a never-ending journey, decluttering is actually an ever-expanding journey. I'll give you an example.

I worked with a client named Lily two years ago. We did 10 days straight, eight hours a day, in her 3,000-square foot house. We released several truckloads of stuff. We sorted a bunch of emotions about her mom's impending death. We made the pantry a thing of beauty and the laundry room worthy of her soul. We uncovered some grief from her teenage years in a box of old letters. We identified her desire to put more energy into art, and less into work. It was a great gig. She felt lighter and inspired, and more in touch with where her soul wanted to go and how to get there.

A year later, Lily called me back to declutter the next layer. A friend said to me, "Jeez, you're going back? Isn't she done yet?" He didn't understand how decluttering really works. In the time since we had done our first round, all kinds of magic had happened. Lily had gracefully made it through her mom's death. She had relinquished her role in her business, risking the end of a decade-long friendship with her partner.

She began painting. She was eating healthier and treating her body better. Her relationship with her husband had deepened. She was more aware of when her ego was at the wheel. Lots had changed. And she was ready for the next round, based on where she was now.

Decluttering is about listening for our soul's longing in present time, over time. So we dove back in. We emptied the no longer relevant paperwork from her file cabinet to create space for a new artistic pursuit; a book she wanted to write. We transformed an unused space into a workout room, because now that she was eating better, she wanted to exercise more. We easily released a bunch of old clothes in the garage that she was unwilling to part with before.

We sorted some new emotions about family life without her mom. We honored her husband by taking her books out of his office bookshelf, symbolically pulling her energy out of his space to make room for him. We acknowledged the new opportunities that had come to her and her ex-business partner/still best friend. We did another pass through the areas where she had re-accumulated; the laundry room, some feelings of insecurity, and the shoe department in her closet. We identified where her ego mind still tried to be the navigator of her life. All in all, another successful decluttering adventure.

This is how it goes. As we declutter, we identify more with our true nature. We begin to spot when our ego mind grabs the wheel. We feel better because stuck energy starts to flow. New inner and outer things that are in alignment with our soul come into our lives. And we often re-accumulate in certain areas. Re-accumulating is a natural part of the decluttering process. Remember, ego patterns of acquiring are ingrained in us, and reinforced by the marketing-driven society we live in that says we're not enough, don't have enough, and need more. Because of this, clearing clutter takes awareness and practice. But the rewards keep coming, making the journey enjoyable and, without a doubt, worthwhile.

I always say decluttering is like buying a one-way ticket. Once we're onboard, every stop on the journey changes our awareness and changes us. Every stop helps us reclaim ourselves and our space a bit more. Every stop holds some magic and possibility that leads to the next stop. Here's one more example to bring this point home.

> *My client Jim was working the 9-5 grind, doing something he didn't love but it paid the bills. There were beautiful photographs all over his house. His photographs. As we worked, he mentioned he had abandoned this passion somewhere along the way. Then we cleared out the basement. As we removed the last of the stuff, he said, "Oh my god, this could be a perfect photography studio!" He couldn't see this possibility before. Taking action in the basement led to a flash of soul inspiration; the previously uninhabitable space in the basement could now be inhabited by his previously uninhabited inner artist. Both were given new life. What happens next is part of the mystery of it all. But with our souls leading the way, we can be certain we're headed in the right direction.*

Because we are of two minds and move in and out of ego and soul consciousness, decluttering never ends. I don't find that daunting or discouraging. I think it actually takes the pressure off. As we remain dedicated to our freedom, decluttering becomes a way of being, rather than a task to complete. Over time, more and more is revealed about our clutter and our soul, and life changes bit by beautiful bit. Now you may be thinking, *well that's not what I was looking for when I bought this book.* And that may be true; this book may not be the book for you right now. But I would ask you to give it a chance. People buy a decluttering book because their soul is calling to them: "Free yourself! Free yourself!" Very often though, the book sits unread on the (cluttered) bookshelf. With any luck, the person reads some of it and incorporates some strategies, and their life changes a bit. This is a win! But then the ego takes the wheel again.

In my work, I've decluttered more books on decluttering than you can imagine. That is not a criticism of them. Every book out there has love behind it, great information, and helpful techniques. A few of them have informed my approach to decluttering. The difference with this book is that it identifies the nature of the ego and how it works. Knowing the ego for what it is gives us space to enjoy the ride, celebrate soul victories as they come, and have compassion for when we get stuck. There are all kinds of cool things to experience on the road of the soul. If you want to come along, the next chapter covers some things we need to bring on the trip.

TWO

ESSENTIAL SKILLS:
PRESENCE, MINDFULNESS, RESONANCE,
INSPIRED ACTION

We are not human beings having a spiritual experience.
We are spiritual beings having a human experience.
—Pierre Teilhard de Chardin

To free ourselves from clutter, we have to hold the big picture of ourselves as souls, and notice moment by moment if we're asleep at the wheel or awake. Every moment is an opportunity to shift from the **scared** of the ego, which creates clutter, to the **sacred** of the soul, where clutter can't exist. How do we get from here to there? With presence, mindfulness, resonance, and inspired action. These are must-have skills for the decluttering journey. I introduce each of them here and weave them into the chapters ahead.

Presence
The ego mind does its best to keep us located in the past or the future, rather than the present. It does this by feeding us a steady stream of thoughts about things that have already happened or might happen. For example, when you're ruminating about something that took place last week, criticizing yourself for what you just did, or re-doing conversations with people in your head, ego thoughts are pulling you to the past. When you're worrying about what might happen tomorrow, planning your next move, or rehearsing what you will say in response to the person you are "listening to," ego thoughts are pulling you to the future. Even if you think you are present, your ego may actually be evaluating the moment rather than experiencing it. You might hear yourself

say "Oh look at this beautiful sunset ... it reminds me of that one in Hawaii last summer, just not as nice."

Ego thoughts come one after the other, relentlessly and randomly, bouncing us all over in time. First you're regretting that greasy pizza you ate for lunch; then you're obsessing that your son's life will be over if he doesn't get into that private kindergarten; next you're fuming about how inconsiderate your husband was last night; and now you're thinking your thighs are too chunky for anyone to ever love you.

To experience how your ego mind operates, take a few minutes and simply listen to the voice in your head. Say the thoughts that come in your mind out loud, or write them down, or record them on your phone. This will help you see very clearly how your ego keeps you in a trance, swerving all over the road and heading nowhere fast.

While the ego is doing its thing, the soul is chilling in the background, waiting patiently for some time at the wheel. Where is it waiting? In the present moment. Let's see if we can find it using this simple technique. Say to yourself "I am present right now." Chances are you'll quickly notice you aren't! Repeat the phrase as many times as you have to, until you notice some of the telltale signs of coming into the present, like your thoughts begin to slow down. Your eyes relax, softening your gaze. You involuntarily take a deeper breath. Your body starts to feel heavier. You hear sounds you weren't aware of, like the hum of the refrigerator or children playing outside. You feel more quiet and centered inside.

When we drop into the present moment, our ego thoughts, and the emotion and energy they carry, temporarily dissolve. The reckless driver relinquishes the wheel and we come into connection with ourselves, rather than the imaginary places our ego likes to frequent. Coming present is the first essential skill for decluttering, because the present is where soul consciousness resides. In the present moment, we find ourselves beyond our worries, our wants, our needs, and our past and future. Suddenly the conflict with your friend that was all consuming two minutes ago is less concerning, the cold sore on your lip is no longer a horror, your ex's incredible Instagram life doesn't matter, your student loans aren't paralyzing you with fear, and that gadget you absolutely had to buy yesterday doesn't seem like a game-changer anymore.

In the present moment, we're momentarily peaceful and untroubled. We feel content, maybe even joyful, and definitely grateful. We sense our wholeness, like we *are* enough and we *have* enough. The energy tied up in the activity of our thoughts is liberated, and for a moment, we are free. It's no wonder the present moment is the archenemy of the ego mind!

Most of us don't make a conscious effort to come into the present. We just seem to randomly pop out of default ego mode. It might happen when something beautiful, like a spectacular waterfall or a soaring hawk, grabs your attention. Or when you notice the cool breeze on your skin or glimpse the vulnerability in your aging parents. It might happen in a mundane moment, as you're petting your cat or putting a Band-Aid on your daughter's boo-boo or singing along to your favorite song. Or when you're running down a trail or sitting with the pain in your friend's heart. In these glorious moments, we come out of the trance of our ego mind and into contact with something greater than our worried, self-conscious, separate small selves. It's like our soul eyes open, time disappears, and our awareness expands to feel our place in the family of things. In these moments, we're in the territory of our soul. It feels familiar. It feels right. It's immediately recognizable, even though it's fleeting.

Ironically, we tend to experience these moments of presence as an altered state. But the truth is, the constant past and future focus of the ego mind is the altered state. The way we feel in the present moment—alive, peaceful, safe, grateful, content, connected, and awake to life— is our true nature.

When we are present, we're no longer just our ego minds. This threatens the ego, which is terrified of losing its identity. It fights to take back the wheel, feeding us more thoughts as if to say, *that's not the truth, get back here where you belong.* And that's how the ride goes. Ego vying for the wheel, and soul waiting to be recognized. Most moments we are not present. The good news is there are many, many moments. Each and every one offers an opportunity to get our souls back in the driver's seat. So try it again. Put your attention on the statement "I am present right now." Say it until you arrive at the peaceful place underneath your ego chatter. Notice how good it feels to be momentarily free of the exhausting turbulence of your ego mind. Practice the skill of presence as often as you can remember, and over time, you'll string together more and more moments.

Mindfulness (Can I Get a Witness?)

There is a particular type of presence, called mindfulness, which is the second essential skill for decluttering. Being mindful means becoming an observer, or a witness, of our thoughts, emotions, energies, ways of relating, and actions. As the witness, we have an experience and simultaneously observe that experience without judgment. When you observed your ego thoughts earlier, you were practicing mindfulness. Rather than being your thoughts, you stepped back and watched them and listened to them. You had the experience of them and studied the experience at the same time. Paying attention in this way created some space between you and your thoughts. You could see that one aspect of yourself was thinking. But if it were your only aspect, you couldn't observe it. The aspect of yourself that watches, that witnesses, is your soul.

Mindfulness matters for decluttering because the ego depends on us not being present and not seeing clearly. As the witness, we're less likely to go careening down the road with our egos at the wheel. For example, if you're observing closely, you might notice you're entranced by a thought that isn't really true, or lost in an emotion that doesn't serve you, or experiencing an energy that doesn't feel good, or taking an action that isn't true to your nature. As the witness, we don't judge what we see, we're just grateful that we're present enough to see it. It means we are in a space of awareness, and in that space lies the opportunity for choice. If we can notice the thoughts, feelings, energies, and actions that are with us in a given moment, we're free to choose if they're the ones we want to be with.

In the space of awareness, our soul gets to weigh in on how we want to think, feel, or act. It gives us information in the form of feelings, images, words, body sensations, and intuitive knowings that guide us toward soul-affirming choices. Here's an example of mindfulness in action.

I was with Elizabeth, a new decluttering client. She was nervously flitting around the family room, saying she didn't know where to start. There was a large couch in the room that was stacked with piles of baby clothes in every color and size. I stood her in front of the couch and placed her in the position of observer by asking, "What happens when you look at this couch?" She stood there for about ten seconds, being the witness, noticing her experience.

Then she burst into tears. She said, "When I really stop and look, it's like seeing it for the first time." This is what observing does; it gives us new eyes.

Elizabeth told me she had a five-year-old son and had begun trying for a second child soon after he was born. The clothes were for this next child. But she had suffered several miscarriages and unsuccessful in-vitro treatments along the way. Her eyes again filled with tears and she said, "I don't want to try anymore. I just want to be grateful for what I have. I want to be here for him instead of focused on a child that may never come." Becoming the witness created space. Her ego mind quieted down, and her soul's wisdom, already present within her, came forth clear as a bell.

As we develop our ability to have an experience and notice the experience at the same time, without judgment, we interrupt the habitual programming of our ego and make room for the loving intelligence of our soul. As you declutter, you'll have many opportunities to practice the skill of mindfulness. When you forget to observe, fear not. There will always be another moment to step back and become the witness.

Resonance

The third essential skill for decluttering has to do with energy. Most people are either unaware of energy or deny it exists, but tuning into energy is key on the road trip we are taking. What differentiates one form of energy from another is the speed at which it vibrates, or its frequency. The natural energetic state of our soul is vibrant, which literally means vibrating very rapidly. When our soul is at the wheel, we experience high vibration energies such as love, enthusiasm, gratitude, peace, joy, compassion, contentment, and acceptance. To get a sense of these energies, think about how you feel when you're at your best at work, or singing along to your favorite song, or leaving the gym after a great workout, or picking up shells on the beach. Remember the feeling of being at a spiritually significant place, or sitting down to a neat, organized desk, or meeting a baby (or a puppy!) on your morning walk. These are moments when your energy is a match to who you really are. In contrast, when our egos are at the wheel, we experience lower vibrations of energy, such as irritation, frustration, overwhelm, ambivalence, or urgency. These vibrations may be very familiar, but they are not our natural state.

Vibration matters because our energy is like a radio signal we broadcast to the world. It syncs up with energy of a similar vibration, for better or for worse. Here's how it works. If you're hanging out in the low vibration energies of your ego, you'll sync up with similar ego energies in the world. For example, when you're in the energy of anger, you walk through the world agitated, looking for a fight. And you find one (or two, or ten) because you are transmitting and receiving that resonance. In contrast, if you're hanging out in the high vibration energies of your soul, you'll sync up with similar soul energies in the world. For example, when you're inhabiting the energy of gratitude, you walk through the world with a smile, appreciative and excited about whatever comes your way. And good things come your way, because you are transmitting and receiving that resonance.

This is how our vibration creates our reality. It's not magical thinking, it's just the truth of resonance. It works in the other direction too. Our vibration is also affected by what's out there in the world, for better or for worse. It lowers in response to ego energies we encounter and raises in response to soul energies we encounter. To see this in action, pay attention to how your energy drops when you hear people arguing, or enter a messy bedroom, or get too involved in the evening news. Notice how your energy lifts when someone gives you a hug, or you collaborate successfully with your co-worker, or your dog goes crazy with joy when you take out the leash.

Energy syncing happens whether we're aware of it or not. That's why we have to pay attention to vibration. You already know how. You've observed energy before. You've said things like "My energy feels low today," or "That painting is so inspiring," or "Wow, that woman has amazing energy," or "It feels so good in here," or "That guy creeps me out." The way you feel lets you know whether an energy in yourself, someone else, or your environment is in alignment with your soul nature. If it makes you feel good, it's a helpful energy for you. If it doesn't, it likely isn't. As you declutter, you'll have many opportunities to practice the skill of resonance and tune into the best vibes for you.

Inspired Action

With the skills of presence, mindfulness, and resonance along for the ride, we're better able to contact the soul clarity already present within us. This spurs us on to inspired action, which is the last skill we need for the decluttering journey. The word inspire means to move with divine agency and power. This is exactly the way to declutter. We want to take action with soul-centered joy, certainty, and ease, rather than suffering and struggling. Releasing what isn't really us, and claiming what is, is a celebration after all!

Most people think decluttering is about forcing themselves to get rid of things against their will. But what actually happens in the process is that things **let go of us**. With a clear intention and our souls at the wheel, inner and outer stuff that doesn't serve us reveals itself in a way it couldn't before. And the moment we see something for what it is, its grip loosens. It loses its importance, its necessity, its function, its charge, its power. It gently releases **us**. For example, you might suddenly wake up to the fact that all those little hotel shampoos in the bathroom cabinet don't really help you live your best life and decide to donate them to the local shelter. You might have an epiphany that talking down to your friend makes you **both** feel small and then change your tone in the moment. You might realize that the guilt you're carrying from your dad's death is keeping you from being present with your own son and lay it to rest. Here's an example of inspired action from a client.

> *Claire had a large closet in her home devoted to gift wrapping. It was essentially a mini Hallmark store with small plastic drawers of ribbon, color coded and organized by width. Larger drawers filled with gift cards and gift tags and gift bows. Shelves lined with gift bags of all sizes, complete with matching tissue paper. Endless tubes of wrapping paper for every occasion. You get the picture.*
>
> *On the first day of decluttering, Claire opened the door, looked in, and proclaimed she needed everything in there. Then she half-heartedly took out a few ribbons and some wrinkled wrapping paper, put them in the giveaway bag, and shut the door. The best leader follows, so I went with it.*
>
> *The next day, she was ready to revisit Hallmark. As we stood there, mindfully being with the closet, she said, "I always make a big effort to*

*acknowledge everyone with really thoughtful, pretty gifts." Then she started
to cry and whispered, "I wish someone would acknowledge me that way."
Getting mindful gave her soul a chance to speak a deep longing. She understood she was giving in hopes of receiving.*

*Once we shined a light on the possibility Claire could directly acknowledge
herself, things were ready to let go of her. Suddenly we were in everything
must go mode, when just yesterday the store was closed. With a whoosh,
wrapping paper, bows, ribbons, and gift bags came flying out of the closet.
There was no second-guessing, no what-ifs, and no self-recrimination. She
was almost giddy. When I asked if she was sure, she looked me right in the
eye and said, "Definitely." At least 50 percent of the stuff in the closet let go
of her and went on to a new home.*

This is how decluttering works. Things let go of **you** when they are ready.
That's why there is no need to force anything. Just move along gently and
joyfully, trusting your own timing. And give yourself permission to keep anything you're unsure about. When the time is right, it will release easily. This
is true for all forms of clutter.

One more thing about inspired action. Everything we hold onto is stagnant energy, or said more positively, <u>untapped</u> energy. In other words, there is
vitality stuck in our stuffed cabinets and sad stories and suppressed emotions
and locked up storage units, just waiting to be liberated. When we declutter,
this energy becomes available to us.

As one client said after a release party in her linen closet: "Wow, it's like a
big wave of motivation came through me as all those old sheets left. Let's keep
going!" Harnessing liberated energy keeps us moving along, releasing and
making room for more of what we want for our lives. Also, when we clear even
a little bit of clutter, space is created for new energy to flow in. Unexpected
things tend to happen. For example, you might hear from a long lost relative,
or get a new business opportunity, or start singing again, or feel more alive
than you have in a long time. Pay attention to the magic that happens. It's
loving evidence you are on the right road.

As you declutter, your ego mind will try to keep you uninspired. It
will tell you all kinds of reasons you can't live your true nature and become

clutter-free. All of the reasons will be a lie. It's not too much to do and it's not too hard. It's not too late. You're not too old or too young or too busy. You're not alone, with no one to help with the heavy stuff. You can find little pockets of time, even if you're a single parent with three kids and a full-time job. You won't lose anything or anyone if you decide to clear out the attic of your home or the basement of your heart. In fact, the whole world will benefit from you releasing the clutter that obscures your beautiful soul.

Summary

Most of us spend our days asleep at the wheel, unknowingly driven by our ego mind. Pinballing thoughts, turbulent emotions, low vibration energies, disharmony, and holding on are not our natural states of being. Our true state of being is marked by presence, peace, contentment, acceptance, connection, collaboration, love, and letting go.

Decluttering is an invitation for the awake mind of the soul to take the wheel of our lives. Presence, mindfulness, resonance, and inspired action are the skills that keep our souls in the driver's seat. With practice, we get better at seeing ego thoughts, feelings, energies, and actions for what they are. As we learn to treat the ego aspect of ourselves with compassion, the inner and outer things that are not a match to our true nature begin to release. With our soul as the navigator of our lives, we're on the road to freedom; free to know ourselves as we truly are, live in integrity with our true nature, love the world, and let it love us back. The truth is, we are enough. Other beings are enough. There is enough. As we meet the world this way, we experience a different world.

Now that we have a sense of where we're going and why, it's time to take a deeper dive into the process of decluttering. Next I share the structure I use to help my clients pull themselves out of the quicksand of overwhelm and fear, and into soul-affirming action. As you use it, clutter will begin to let go of you. You'll experience more clarity and peace. Your energy, and the energy of your environments, will shift to a higher vibration. Your relationships will become more loving and harmonious. Your home will transform from a dumping ground for stuff to a soul sanctuary. Space will be created for new things, things of your soul, to come into your life.

Before we move forward, it's important to note that everyone has a different threshold for stuff. There is no one size fits all in the decluttering process. In terms of physical clutter, for example, every possession I own fits in my car, and it's a coupe! That works for me. And I know many perfectly content decluttering souls who have much more. As you identify with your true self, the one beyond your ego mind and the consciousness of society, you'll find your **own** sweet spot. Here, your inner and outer environments will reflect your true nature and have the perfect amount of stuff for you.

THREE

WHERE ARE YOU RIGHT NOW?

This place where you are right now, God circled on a map for you.
—Hafiz

Let's take some time to assess how clutter shows up in your life. This isn't a test and there are no right answers. It's simply an exercise to see where you are right now.

Mental Clutter

- I have difficulty quieting my mind.
- I struggle against life.
- I spend a lot of time thinking about the past or worrying about the future.
- I judge myself and others harshly.
- I hold onto beliefs that might not be true.
- The words I use and the stories I tell support my false self.
- I've lost touch with my intuition, or don't heed it.

Emotional Clutter

- I feel anxious, sad, angry, or lonely a lot.
- I don't do emotions.
- I hide my feelings from those closest to me.
- My emotions get the best of me.
- I have unfinished business with people in my life.
- People walk on eggshells around me, afraid I will discharge my emotions on them.

- My heart is grieving.

Energetic Clutter
- I often feel indecisive, unfocused, or disconnected.
- My energy is easily influenced by the energy of other people.
- My physical environments are draining, overwhelming, chaotic, or agitating.
- The pace and rhythm of my life doesn't really suit me.
- I'm always wanting, needing, striving, or pushing.
- There's too much noise in my life, inside and out.
- I'm constantly in overdrive or I feel stuck and unable to take action.

Relationship Clutter
- I often feel less than, not good enough, or unworthy.
- I have a hard time accepting myself and others.
- I have a lot of bad habits.
- I say yes to things that aren't good or right for me.
- I spend more than I earn or I earn less than I'm worth.
- I rarely spend time in nature.
- I don't feel connected to the people in my life who have passed.

Physical Clutter
- I focus on what I don't have, rather than what I do have.
- I purposely avoid certain areas of my home because they stress me out.
- I often leave things undone.
- I keep a lot of things I don't use just in case I need them.
- I have similar items in different places around the house.
- I have lots of things in my home that I don't really love.
- My house or office or car or garage or purse or wallet has too much stuff in it.

Breathe now. It takes courage to look at what clutters your soul, and how a cluttered soul lives. You can only make changes if you are willing to take an honest look. Maybe you found some surprises in there, or simply confirmation of what you already know. Accept what is right now with love. It is what it is. Judging yourself won't change it. Presence, mindfulness, resonance and inspired action will. Wherever you are in your life right now, there is a distinct, quantum shift available to you. You have the capacity to change your state of mind from one that creates clutter to one in which clutter can no longer exist.

FOUR

UNCOVERING YOUR SOUL'S LONGING

No problem can be solved from the same level of consciousness that created it.
—*Albert Einstein*

Now that you have a clearer picture of where you are, let's take a look at where your soul might want to go. Take a few minutes to consider these questions:

- What would be different in your life if you allowed yourself to be guided by your true nature?
- What kinds of thoughts would you think?
- What emotions would you feel?
- What kind of energy would you put forth in the world?
- Who would you be in your relationships, and which relationships would you be in?
- What would you do more of, and what would you do less of?
- What would your home or your office or the trunk of your car look like?

Decluttering is an ongoing process of defining what our souls are longing for in present time, over time. So let's get curious about what your soul desires right now. To do this, it's important to make the distinction between an ego mind desire and a soul desire. An ego mind desire usually highlights something we think needs to be "fixed." For example, an ego mind desire might be *I have to lose 20 pounds*. In contrast, a soul desire doesn't highlight a problem, it reveals a possibility. The soul version would be more like *I'm vibrant, fit, and alive in my body*. See the difference? More importantly, can you FEEL the difference? As I write this book, my soul desire is *I share what I've learned to help others*. It feels dynamic and positive. It's grounded in what's important to me right now. It makes me feel relaxed and excited at the same time. Here are other examples from some of my clients:

> *I feel spacious, connected, and on purpose.*
> *I have a solid foundation, mental clarity, and clear space.*
> *I operate with ease and efficiency in my life.*
> *I'm doing my art again.*
> *My life is harmonious and peaceful.*
> *I connect with myself, others, and nature.*
> *I engage joyfully and gratefully with life.*
> *I'm grounded and in the flow.*
> *My business thrives and helps people.*
> *I have room to grow.*
> *I honor my grief, put it to rest, and live again.*
> *I'm light, bright, relaxed, and engaged.*
> *I give and receive love freely.*
> *I live an honest life.*

Let's take some time to consult with **your** inner wise self about what it's longing for right now. Sit quietly and allow your mind to slow down. Take a deep breath and settle into your bones and heart and stomach and being. Then ask to be shown what your soul deeply desires for the next year of your life. The answer may come to you in an image, or through words, a body sensation, or a feeling. Trust whatever comes, even if it surprises you. You'll recognize a desire that springs from your soul because your heart will open, and it will feel **right**. Once you identify it, fine tune it and write it down.

The next step is to make your soul desire real in your mind. Your subconscious mind can't distinguish between something real and something imagined. So say your desire out loud. Imagine you are already living it. Experience it in as much detail as possible. See it, feel it in your body, smell it, hear it, taste it. Feel the emotions of it. Feel the energy of it. Become it. Notice the difference in your vibration. This is key. Imagine yourself gliding through your home and your life, your soul desire and its vibration rippling out from within. Embodying your soul desire in this way transforms it into your soul intention.

Once you identify your current soul's desire, experience it, and feel its vibration, it's yours to have. You've given your mind and energetic system a new intention and resonance, direct from your soul self. From here on out, you don't need to focus on fixing your clutter problem or forcing yourself to get rid of stuff. The more elegant way to declutter is to keep your soul intention at the forefront of your mind, as if it's already happening. Focusing there will open the door to a new reality. As you hold the big picture of yourself as a soul, and locate in your soul intention moment by moment, things in your inner and outer spaces that aren't in alignment will become obvious and begin to release. The next few chapters offer some tools to support where your soul wants to go.

FIVE

THE ROADMAP

Re-examine all that you have been told ... dismiss that which insults your soul.
—*Walt Whitman*

The questions below are the roadmap for your decluttering journey. Ask them about everything in your life and listen very closely to the answers. If you follow this map, the things in your life that are in alignment with your soul, and the things that aren't, will begin to reveal themselves. And you'll be on the road to freedom.

Does it contribute to my soul intention?

Does this thought, feeling, energy, way of relating, or possession contribute to your soul intention? For example, does it help you feel *spacious*, or live with *ease and efficiency*, or feel *light, bright, relaxed and engaged*. This question cuts directly to what's essential. It's really the only question you need to declutter. A **no** answer to this question indicates it's time to let something go. Easy enough, but your ego mind will make it complicated. It will examine and refute and fret and fuss. It will do its best to keep you holding onto things that don't contribute to your soul intention. The rest of the questions will help you make decisions that support your soul's knowing.

Is it beautiful?

Is this thought, feeling, energy, way of relating, or possession beautiful? This is simple enough, but one caveat here. You may be able to say, "Yes, that is a beautiful abstract painting," but if you prefer realist paintings, it would be a candidate for release. As would anything else that isn't in alignment with **your** soul's preference for beauty. If it isn't beautiful to YOU, let it go.

Is it useful?

Is this thought, feeling, energy, way of relating, or possession useful? You're looking for the things that contribute to your effectiveness in life and empower you to do the things your soul wants to do. This question seems self-explanatory but be aware when answering. You may say, "Well, this belief that I need everyone's approval has helped me stay safe in my life, so yes, it is useful," but the truth is it keeps you from living life your way. Or you may say, "Yes, these ski poles are very useful," but the truth is you stopped skiing years ago. Be clear that whatever it is, it's truly useful to live your soul's intention now. If it's not useful to you, let it go.

Does it love me back?

Does this thought, feeling, energy, way of relating, or possession love you back? The things you love and that love you back make your heart sing. They feel good. In their presence, your energy lights up and you say, "Oh, I LOVE that!"

Get curious if the things in your life evoke that kind of feeling. Or, are they more like the vase your ex-husband's parents gave you; the ugly yellow one with the little red hummingbirds that makes you cringe each time you see it? Or the feeling of shame that comes over you when you compare your body to the airbrushed models in the magazines? Or your frustration when the random stuff jammed in the hall closet falls every time you take out the vacuum? These are examples of things that don't love you back. They hit you with an energy current that isn't true to you. It's not wise to subject yourself to that repeatedly. If it doesn't love you back, let it go.

Is it in present time?

Is this thought, feeling, energy, way of relating, or possession in present time? Most of us don't live in present time. We either locate in past time, which is the land of memories, outdated beliefs, or charged emotions from other times and places; or in future time, which is the land of fear and planning. If you hang out in past time, you'll notice yourself thinking and talking a lot about the days of yore. You might glorify old relationships, or lament how you used to be a size six, or repeatedly tell stories of the trials and tribulations of your life. You'll have skinny clothes in your closet, a file cabinet that barely opens, and regret that you didn't say yes to that job offer five years ago. You'll feel guilty or sad or angry more often than you care to admit.

If you hang out in future time, you'll find yourself focusing on what might happen. You'll plan ahead to the point of missing the moment or be hypervigilant about everything so you can manage any impending disasters. You'll helicopter everyone in your life and pride yourself on anticipating "their" needs. You'll have fat clothes in your closet, an overabundance of worry, and lots of brown grocery bags stuffed in the space between the refrigerator and kitchen cabinet. You'll be prepared for any eventuality, and hear yourself saying things like "I have to keep this, just in case," or "I might need that someday," or "What if…?"

Remember, the ego does its best to keep us in past and future time. But our soul is at home in present time, dancing with life as it is, moment by moment. When we live in present time, our physical environments reflect who we are now, and what our life is now. We're willing to experience moments as they come, without rushing ahead or holding on. We trust that everything we truly need comes to us in the perfect time and the best way, and that we have, and have always had, the flexibility and capacity to respond to whatever happens in our life. If something is not in present time, let it go.

Does it have a sacred place to live?

Does this thought, feeling, energy, way of relating, or possession have a sacred place to live? Think of it this way. Of all the things in this great big world, you've chosen **this** particular thing to fill your inner or outer spaces. The fact that you've chosen it automatically makes it sacred. Therefore, you must honor it and appreciate its service to you. You must ensure that it has a sacred place to live. If it is a possession, treat it with respect by keeping it and the place it lives clean and neat. Even if it's relegated to a drawer or a closet or a cabinet in the garage, be sure it's easy to see, easy to get to, and easy to find. If it's a thought, feeling, energy, or relationship you choose to keep, it too should be given a place of honor. It must be visible, accessible, and appreciated. A decluttered soul lives transparently, with everything in its right place. If you can't find a sacred place for something to live, let it go.

Does it help me serve my love to the world?

Does this thought, feeling, energy, way of relating, or possession help you serve your love to the world? We are here to be of service by sharing our love. Your soul knows the unique ways **you** are meant to love. You've always had a certain way, certain skills, certain gifts, and certain dreams about who you wanted to be and what you wanted to do. When you're sharing your love with the world, you know it. Your heart is open, alive with intention and purpose. You're in your natural flow, with nothing damming up the river of your focus and energy. You're receiving more than you could ever give. If something in your inner or outer spaces doesn't help you serve your love to the world, it no longer serves you. Let it go.

SIX

GETTING STARTED

A journey of a thousand miles begins with a single step.
—*Lao Tzu*

Start Somewhere

"I don't know where to start!" I hear this one a lot. Most people are overwhelmed by their clutter and can't imagine where to begin. The good news is that it doesn't matter where you begin, because it's all connected! Every action you take, in either your inner or outer environments, is significant. A shift in one area elegantly affects every other area. The key is to start somewhere. Let your intuition tell you the best place for YOU to begin. It might direct you to your office cabinets. It might lead you to a certain area of your heart. It might flash an image of someone in your life. Go where your intuition guides you, be it a particular room of your home or a particular corner of your mind or a particular aspect of your behavior. Allow the questions to permeate your being. *Does this contribute to my soul's intention? Is it beautiful? Is it useful? Does it love me back? Is it in present time? Does it have a sacred place to live? Does it help me serve my love to the world?*

Whether it's a thought or a feeling or an energy or a relationship or a possession, some things belong to you, some things belong to others, some are ready to be reabsorbed into the universe, and some are ready for disposal. Have your literal and symbolic bags ready. One for giveaway, one for recycling, and one for throwaway. And then begin.

Do It Your Way

"I don't know how to do it!" I hear this one a lot as well. There is no right way to declutter. The only "rule" is to feel good as you do it. Some of the strategies

I've discovered in my travels are listed below. Try them on for size and see which work for you. Trust your intuition about the best strategy in any given moment. Be solid in where you're going (your soul intention), and flexible in how you get there.

Decluttering Strategies:

- Make a daily practice, a meditation if you will, and release five things per day.
- Take 10 minutes while your coffee is brewing to declutter a drawer, or pay a bill you've been putting off, or clear the negative energy that lodged in your belly after the scene with your daughter last night.
- Set aside a few hours and clear a clutter zone, such as the bathroom cabinets or a tricky relationship. Take that same chunk of time to do something that supports your soul self, like reading that book about healing grief or starting that art project or taking your sister to lunch to let her know how much you appreciate her.
- Walk through your living room or your relationships or your daily habits and cherry pick the things that no longer speak to you, such as those worn-out pillows, or your tendency to keep score, or your third morning cigarette.
- Go into your kitchen cabinets, pull out everything that loves you back and put it on the counter, then see what's left for release.
- For five consecutive days, use 15 minutes of your lunch break to clear your office files or pen a letter of gratitude to your dad.
- Take a weekend and let your soul self clean out the garage.
- Find 30 minutes after work to do something soul-affirming, like being in nature, writing in your journal, or riding your bicycle.
- Release 25 things each day, for seven days straight. Anything counts, whether it's one of the many pieces of paper littering your desk, an old soccer ball from the garage, the candy you secretly consume at night, or your habit of saying "I'm sorry" too much. Enjoy your surprise when it's easier than you think.

- Schedule a stay-cation and tackle the basement, or any family secrets that are ready to go public, such as your son's alcohol abuse or your desire to separate from your wife.
- Gather all the similar things in the house, such as books or blankets or photographs, and bring them to a central area for sorting and release.
- Empty your whole closet and put back only what is worthy of coming with you for the next year of your life.
- Schedule an hour or two a week for decluttering and decide in the moment what to focus on.
- Find something you used to love to do, such as cross-country skiing or knitting or reading historical fiction and see if it's truly something essential to your soul in present time. • Link your decluttering to an already established routine. For example, finish dinner, spend 30 minutes clearing, and then watch your favorite show.

Watch for Resistance

When we're tuned into our soul intention, motivation and commitment aren't a problem. Challenges arise when the ego mind activates, which it will. It will offer resistance to decluttering. Resistance is simply the fear of the ego showing itself. It's the ego's attempt to survive. The ego engages in subtle warfare or epic battles, always disguising the fear as something else.

Subtle warfare looks like procrastinating, losing interest, getting impatient, breaking your word to yourself, feeling anxious or mentally foggy, or decluttering half-heartedly. You'll hear yourself thinking or saying things like: "It's too overwhelming," or "I'm too tired from work," or "I just can't concentrate on this right now," or "I'll get to it tomorrow," or "I don't need to look through that box, I already know what's in there."

Epic battles, on the other hand, look like flat-out avoidance, anger or dread about decluttering, a sense of urgency to get it all done, forcing yourself to keep going when you have done enough for the day, getting physically sick, or even sustaining an injury. If you're in an epic battle with your ego mind, you'll hear yourself thinking or saying things like: "I have way too much going on right now to deal with this," or "There's no way I'll ever get through this stuff," or "Big deal I did the closet, look at all the rest of this crap," or "Screw this, what's the point?," or "This book is bullshit," or "Clutter doesn't really bother me," or "I'll never be _____ (fill in your soul intention)." Resistance is a clue that your ego mind is at the wheel, trying to take you down a dead end.

Be grateful when you notice resistance and take a moment to stop and hug your ego mind. If you acknowledge its fear and thank it for trying to help, it will often quiet down and allow you to proceed. If you notice resistance getting the best of you, relax into it rather than forcing your way through it. This is counter-intuitive, but when you surrender, you find your way back to presence and thus to connection with your soul. From there, you can consciously choose the next best action to take. Very often, simply slowing down a bit or redirecting to an area of decluttering that's less charged for you, like the silverware drawer, or taking a body-affirming walk in the park, will get you back on track.

It's important to note that there is a difference between succumbing to ego resistance e.g., "Oh, f*ck it!" and surrendering to it so you can ultimately move forward. Practice identifying that edge within yourself. If you get completely hijacked by your ego mind's trickery, so be it. Accept where you are, take a break, and embrace any uncertainty you feel about decluttering. It may take a few minutes or a few hours or a few days or a few months to get your soul back in the driver's seat, cruising with inspiration again. Trust your timing. Remember, there are two aspects within you; the one that is comfortable in clutter (ego mind) and the one that longs for freedom (soul mind). As you stay dedicated to your freedom, and mindful of how your ego grabs the wheel, clutter clearing will happen in right-sized chunks and pacing for you.

Ride the Waves

As we declutter, we come face to face with our identity, our personal history, and our significant life experiences. It's a **big** deal. Stuff gets stirred up, inside and out. For example, you may experience unexpected emotions like anxiety, grief, or even happiness. You might feel on top of the world one minute, and then inexplicably fall apart the next. You might encounter turbulence in your relationships or fatigue in your physical body. Your home or office might be in disarray; boxes on the floor and projects in process and rooms half-done.

Ride the waves, without struggling or over-analyzing or freaking out. Remember, you are liberating thoughts, emotions, energies, ways of relating, and possessions that have been stuck for a long time. Commit to be with whatever happens as stagnant energy begins to move. Trust it is in service to where your soul wants to go. Remind yourself often: *this too shall pass.* These four words hold deep soul truth about our hardest moments, most joyful moments, and everything in-between. They help us allow moments to come and go without holding on.

Rely on the Magic of 10 Percent

The magic of 10 percent helps us release clutter with ease, because it keeps our ego mind feeling safe. As you declutter, look to release 10 percent of the things that don't contribute to your soul intention, and add 10 percent of the things that do. For example, if you're decluttering your closet, find one shirt out of every 10 that you can part with. Or add 10 percent more beauty by folding your sweaters neatly or by lining up your shoes. Manageable, right? Small changes like this can make a big difference.

The magic of 10 percent works in your inner **and** outer environments. Here are some examples. Release 10 percent of your mean to self thoughts and add 10 percent more self-loving thoughts. Spend 10 percent less time on the couch and 10 percent more time moving your body. Drop your complaints by 10 percent and up your compliments by 10 percent. Engage 10 percent less with people who bring you down and 10 percent more with people who lift you up. Reduce feelings of jealousy by 10 percent and add 10 percent more appreciation. Get the idea?

Here are a few more examples, just to be sure the magic lands. Choose 10 percent less time with others and 10 percent more time with yourself. Eat 10 percent less junk and 10 percent more greens. Reduce screen time by 10 percent and increase nature time by 10 percent. Spend 10 percent less on dining out and add 10 percent more to your savings account.

As you practice the magic of 10 percent, you may notice some areas are easier than others. If you can't part with 10 percent of your jeans but can easily release the old towels in the laundry room or your habit of interfering in your friend's life, then do 20 percent in one of those areas. Aiming for 10 percent makes decluttering fun and do-able, and most people surprise themselves by doing even more. One of my favorite things is to hear a client proudly proclaim, "That was like 40 percent ... whoo hoo!"

Remember, if you're in any way hesitant to release something, don't. There will always be another round of decluttering, and you're always changing, so you can trust that when it's truly time for something to let go, it will easily.

Liberate It

If you find something you love enough to keep, or something you're not sure about, *liberate it*. Take it out of the packaging, storage box, back of the closet, corner of your mind, or recess of your heart. Whether it's a new idea, a feeling you haven't allowed yourself to feel, a relationship you're not sure about, or an object, put it into play. Find a place for it. A place out in the open, a prominent place, a place of honor. And then engage with it. Look at it. Feel it. Try it on. Sense its energy. Use it. Explore it. Talk to it. Wear it. Go out to dinner with it. Make something with it. See if it truly feeds your soul. Then you'll know what to do with it.

Off We Go

Now let's delve into the different forms of clutter and ways to free ourselves. The next few chapters cover mental, emotional, energetic, relationship, and physical clutter. It will be most helpful to read them straight through, as they build on each other. However, if you want to jump ahead and read about a particular type of clutter, feel free. Just know that information in a previous section might support your understanding. At the end of each chapter, I mention resources that can help you take a deeper dive into clutter and freedom. More information about them can also be found at the end of the book in the section: Resources and Further Reading.

SEVEN

MENTAL CLUTTER

There is nothing more important to true growth than realizing you
are not the voice of the mind— you are the one who hears it.
—Michael Singer

All clutter ultimately begins with our thoughts. Our thoughts create the emotions we experience, the energy we exude, and the actions we take. The ego mind bombards us with thoughts that are not true to who we really are. Ego thoughts are rooted in self-preservation. They spring from scarcity and lack. They criticize and compare. They constantly categorize: right/wrong, good/bad, superior/inferior. They judge others, desperate to feel separate from them. At the same time, they seek approval and validation, desperate to belong. Ego thoughts all contain some version of *I am not enough, you are not enough, and there is not enough.* And they constantly pull our attention to a past that is already gone, or some imagined future where bad things are certain to happen.

Ego thoughts are mental clutter in and of themselves. When we unwittingly attach to them, other forms of clutter get created. For example, if you latch onto the ego thought *I'm so lonely,* you will find yourself feeling sad and rehashing the betrayals of your life. If you over-identify with the ego thought *I have to prove I'm successful,* you might buy a closet full of clothes you don't need and can't afford. If you repeatedly believe the ego thought *I'll never have enough money,* you might trudge along in a job you hate, counting the years to retirement.

A good time to see your ego thoughts in action is in the morning, upon waking. Watch how you emerge from sleep feeling tranquil, and then

vroom! your mental engine revs up with thought after thought. Mine activates with stuff like: *ugh ... I'm gonna freeze up in the meeting today and look like
an idiot* or *If I don't get some new clients soon I'm gonna die penniless on the streets.*
Then I'm replaying a scene from yesterday, rehearsing the lines I should have
said to put that guy in his place. Then I'm thinking *hmmm, my ankle feels
stiff, there must be something really wrong in there* as I see myself on the gurney
heading into the amputation surgery. Then I'm in a mental rant about the
outrageous stuff going on with the Royal Family, then I'm running through
my to-do list for the day (that I don't want to do), and then I'm imagining
what it will be like when my parents die and I am alone **and** dealing with
crepey skin. And then I'm bouncing through a bunch of random thoughts
about writing this book: *I suck at writing. It's way too hard and I'll never finish. No one will publish it because they are too stupid to get it and I don't even care
anyway.* Suffice it to say, the morning thought parade reveals the cluttered
mess in our heads.

In fact, we're so accustomed to our thoughts, we don't stop to consider
their source. We think we **are** our thoughts. We assume that because we're
thinking them, they must be true. We're seduced and compelled by them. We
spin stories and create drama to defend them. We hurt ourselves in service to
them. We project them onto other people. We can even believe our thoughts
to the degree that we're willing to physically harm another person.

The good news is there's another mental reality, based in our inherent
soul nature of peace, harmony, trust, and acceptance. Remember, the ego is
part of our human experience, but it's not all of who we are. We can invite our
souls to take the wheel and travel a new road.

To release the mental clutter of the ego mind and shift into the mental
freedom of the soul, rely on and practice presence, mindfulness, resonance, and
inspired action. Hold up whatever you find in your mental closet to the light
of the questions: *Does this thought or way of thinking contribute to my soul intention?
Is it beautiful? Is it useful? Does it love me back? Is it in present time? Does it have
a sacred place to live? Does it help me serve my love to the world?* Dealing with ego
thoughts is the most challenging task of our human existence. But don't let
that scare you! Have fun getting to know your mental clutter and watching
it release.

Come Present

Releasing mental clutter isn't about getting rid of thoughts. That's impossible, as thoughts keep coming whether we want them to or not. It's also not about fighting against our thoughts, because fighting with the ego mind is a losing battle. The only way to release mental clutter is to come into presence, because mental clutter can't exist in the present moment.

As an example, think of a time when ego thoughts had you in their grip. Maybe it was after an argument with your partner, or when the rent was coming due, or when your doctor gave you some concerning news. Can you recall how your mind ricocheted with thoughts, relentlessly analyzed what happened, and worried about what might happen next? Can you remember the agitation and disturbance inside, as if you couldn't stop thinking? Being absorbed in ego thoughts is like bouncing off the walls in a confined space, unable to find the doorway to mental peace.

Chances are in an attempt to get out of your head, you told a friend what was going on in there. And what did that friend say? Yup, that's right: "Don't worry about it ... **just let it go.**" Somewhere inside you knew they were right, but how the hell do you do that? Just the suggestion made your mind spin even more, and left you feeling ashamed that you couldn't find your way out. We've all been there, and we'll all revisit that place many times. It's part of our human condition. But a better way to help ourselves and each other through those moments is to say, "**just be here right now,**" instead of "just let it go." Why? Because the only way to let go, to free ourselves from the grip of our ego mind, is to come present. In presence, the door to mental peace reveals itself.

Coming present is like a superpower that got shoved in the back of our mental closet, forgotten about and unused. Now is the time to bring it out and try it on for size. One way to drop into presence is to practice mental time-outs, which of course are really soul time-ins. The next time you notice your ego mind revving up, practice coming back to neutral by shifting your attention to your senses. See, with your eyes, what's in front of you. Listen, with your ears, for the sounds around you. Smell, with your nose, what's pleasant or otherwise. Feel, with your body, the sensations of blood flowing, bones supporting, the texture of your clothes, the temperature of the air on your skin, or the weight of your body on the chair. Allow yourself to be fully absorbed in all your senses. When we take a mental time-out like this, we drop into presence. This creates a break in the action of our thoughts; a glorious moment of "no-mind," where our soul slips back into the driver's seat. Try it right now and notice how your mind quiets down.

Another helpful way to come present is to rely on your breath. Thoughts, like breath, just come. In and out, without any effort from us. As you breathe in, notice a thought that has arisen in your mind. Simply label it *thinking*. As you exhale, imagine the thought flowing out of your mouth, dissolving into thin air. This keeps your attention in the present moment, letting go rather than attaching to the content of your thoughts.

The present moment is the safest, truest, most natural place to be. In the right now, all is truly well. We're in connection with ourselves, rather than in imaginary places. We're calm and aware, dropped into the energy field that connects all things. We have access to our inner knowing. For a moment, we're at peace, until the next time our ego thoughts activate; five seconds, five minutes, or five hours from now.

To release mental clutter, take inspired action to claim your superpower. Find your way to presence whenever you can remember. With awareness and practice, you'll be able to quiet your ego thoughts at will. No one will know that as you're waiting in line at the grocery store, or sitting with friends at dinner, or listening to a presentation at work, you're letting go of clutter and dropping into your true nature.

Be the Witness

To declutter our mental space, it's essential to become aware of our thoughts. We can observe them as if we're lying on the grass, watching passing clouds. Thoughts are like clouds in that they come and go across our minds. We usually attach to them and follow them blindly to places we don't want to go. But as the witness, we simply observe our thoughts as they come through our mind. We have an experience (our thoughts) and notice that experience at the same time, without judgment. This present moment awareness, or mindfulness, helps us make the distinction between our ego mind and our soul. We notice one aspect of us is thinking, but if it was the only aspect of us, we couldn't observe it. The aspect of us that watches, the witness, is our soul.

Being the witness shines a light on our thoughts; not a harsh light like the hanging bulb in an interrogation room, but a light of awareness and compassion. We're curious about them. We understand they're misguided and afraid. We know they're untrue, and out of present time. We want to accept them for what they are, so we can detach from them and be more free. As we observe our ego thoughts lovingly, without judgment, they naturally quiet down. And we also begin to realize that most of them are not true! This helps us take them less seriously, or even be amused by them. The ego mind offers up thousands of thoughts a day, most of them repetitive. All you have to do is watch.

Inhabit the Space of Choice

Mindfully paying attention to our thoughts naturally slows our thinking down. This creates a little space around our thoughts. In that space lies the opportunity for choice. For example, you might choose to simply let a thought pass by like a cloud. Or you might find your attention attaching to a thought, in which case you can take some time to question it. Is the thought true? Does it contribute to my soul intention? Is it helpful, kind, and loving? Does it elevate my energy? If you get a no answer to your questions, you're in position to consciously choose a different thought, one that's more aligned with your true nature and thus more helpful to you. This is not positive thinking, which many people use to deny or suppress their ego mind. With furrowed brow, clenched jaw, and white knuckles, they say, "No, that negative thought is not me. I'm not going to think about it. I'm going to think about butterflies and unicorns!" And their ego delights in the battle, knowing it will emerge victorious.

True mental freedom comes from welcoming all the thoughts of our ego mind because they're part of us, and then having the presence of (soul) mind to observe them, let them pass by, or question them if they capture our attention. Get familiar with the space of awareness. That's where choice resides. Cultivate it. With practice, ego thoughts will release, leaving room for that which affirms your soul.

Soften into Acceptance

As you observe your ego mind, pay particular attention to thoughts that resist what's happening in any given moment. For example, if it's raining, you may think *I wish it were sunny.* If you're relaxing on the couch you might hear the thought *stop being lazy.* If you're feeling down, you may say to yourself *there are people starving in the world, get over yourself.* If you're snuggling with your partner, you might think *this is okay but I wish she would hold me this way.* When we resist what is, our mind, body, and energy contracts, saying no to what is happening in present time.

Resistance is a major form of mental clutter. It's a clue the ego mind is at the wheel, pushing its agenda of how things should be and keeping us out of the present moment. To release resistant thoughts, witness them without judgment. First, thank your ego for offering its opinion. Then see if you can settle into the space of awareness. In that space, you can choose to say a whole-hearted yes to whatever's happening. Here's an example.

Jodi and I were meeting another friend for lunch. She was late. We sat for a few minutes waiting, and I could see Jodi getting antsy. Then she went into full-on resistance. She started ranting about her dwindling lunch hour, and how lateness makes her crazy because "it's so rude!" Her body began tensing up. She kept leaning forward and glancing at the door every few seconds, and then sitting back in her seat, tapping her fingers on the table. I tried to carry on a conversation with her, but she wasn't really paying attention. At one point she interrupted me and said, "I mean if she really cared about us she'd be here!"

*Since I see every moment as an opportunity to release clutter, and because Jodi is a good friend, I decided a light-hearted intervention was in order. So I gently said, "Jodi, she isn't here … and in your resistance, **neither are you**!" She paused and I could see her wheels turning. Then I said, "C'mon, let's get present." She smirked at me in her Jodi way. I took that as a yes, looked right in her eyes, and said, "I choose to accept what's happening right now." I said it four or five times.*

Then she started giggling and joined me. There we were in the booth, repeating the mantra together. I watched her take a couple of deep breaths and then settle back into her seat with her hands on her lap, coming into the present. Her face softened and her shoulders dropped even more present.

She started looking around the restaurant and said, "Wow, this place is really pretty." (now she's here.) Then, "It's kind of nice to have a moment to chill, it was an intense morning." (easing into acceptance.) We sat quietly for a minute before she added, "I never do this, but I'm gonna go ahead and order so I can enjoy my meal, and when she gets here, she gets here." (ahhhh ... total acceptance.)

Acceptance is the only antidote for mental resistance. When we meet resistance with acceptance, we slip out of the clutches of our ego mind and into the reality of the present. We're no longer hostage to our thoughts. Instead, we're in position to make soul-affirming choices (like Jodi deciding to order) with a relaxed mind and body.

The ego mind perpetually fights against the reality of what is. Notice how you resist small things, such as an unexpected schedule change, or bigger things, such as the fact you got laid off from your job, or your girlfriend left you, or one of your family members is sick. When we resist, we suffer. In fact, all suffering is resistance to what is. That's deep, so take a moment with it. See where it may be true for you. If you look closely, you'll see that most of your perceived problems are really just your ego mind resisting what is. When we accept what is, there's never a problem. There's just what's happening now and how we're dealing with it.

Contrary to popular opinion, surrendering into acceptance is not a choice to stay stuck in a situation we don't like. In fact, it's the opposite. **Resistance is what keeps us stuck.** When we accept what is, our mind clears and the energy we have tied up in resistance is liberated. This leaves us free to access our inner wise self to create solutions. And, in the even bigger picture, a decluttered soul trusts whatever is happening is exactly what should be happening, even if it's not yet clear why. Much of what happens in our life only makes sense when we look at it in the rearview mirror. We resist and struggle in the moment and then find ourselves saying at some point "Oh, it all makes sense now" or "Everything worked out for the best."

Acceptance allows us to enter the natural flow of events rather than trying to control them with our small (ego) perspective of how things should be. So stay mindful of the clutter of resistant thoughts. In the space of awareness, you can choose acceptance, which puts your soul back at the wheel where it belongs, free to meet with grace whatever is happening.

Choose Your Lens

When we believe an untrue ego thought over time, it can solidify into another form of mental clutter: a belief that affirms our false self. A belief is simply a thought we keep thinking and believing. Many of us are driven by ego-based beliefs, such as *I have to achieve to earn love, the world is unsafe, or I'm responsible for other people's feelings.* These beliefs are mental clutter and they create all kinds of other clutter. Here's an example from a client.

Katie was a mom to her 13-year old son Kyle. As we were decluttering her guest room, we came across 10 jumbo plastic bins that contained all of Kyle's artwork and schoolwork from his first day of kindergarten until now. When I asked her about them, she said, "Oh we don't have to go through those, I need to keep them so Kyle can remember his childhood."

When Kyle came home after school, I noticed she started doing everything for him; making him an elaborate snack, helping him take off his football gear, getting his video game ready for him to play. All the while she was asking him question after question about his day. When he mentioned a minor problem he had at school, she jumped in with three solutions. And when he said, "I'm so sore from practice" she said, "Oh, sweetie" three times (with a truly pained expression), and then ran into the bathroom to get an array of ointments. As he ate his snack and played his video game with his headphones on, she applied them.

Later, when Kyle went to his room, I mentioned what I had observed and asked her to describe how she saw their relationship. She said, "His dad and I went through a bad divorce. I couldn't believe he left me. It's just been me and Kyle since then. And I was always afraid I would lose him too." I asked her how all the bins and her caretaking of him related to that. She got quiet for a long time, and then said: "I've just always been afraid he was going to grow up and leave me." There it was. An ego belief that was driving her to keep her son her "little boy." The clutter (the bins of stuff, her fear, her ways of relating with him) was the belief made visible.

The good news was that in this space of awareness, Katie could consider a new, more soul-centered belief like "My son is connected to my heart, in every phase of his life." And she did. A bunch of those bins let go of her in the next few days, as did some feelings of grief and loss about the divorce, and some of her overzealous caretaking. On the last day, I walked in to find Kyle making his first-ever self-made batch of mac and cheese while proudly telling Katie about a problem with his coach he had handled that day by himself. Decluttering miracles never cease! Katie was now on a new road to experience life with Kyle in present time, without holding on or holding him back.

Our beliefs are the lens through which we experience the world. When we look through that lens, we find evidence out there in the world that reinforces the belief. In this way, our life experience is in harmony with our dominant beliefs, for better or for worse. As an example, if you repeatedly believe the ego-based thought *I have to do it all myself,* emotions like stress, overwhelm, and resentment become your norm. Your energy gets urgent and forceful, in order to push through all you "have" to do. You find fault with the way others try to help, because none of it is good enough. Pretty soon people stop offering, which reinforces your belief that you have to do it all yourself. This is your life coming into harmony with your dominant belief. Now if you held the more soul-centered belief *I can rely on others*, life would be different. You would know you're immersed in a web of available support, surrounded by helpers seen and unseen, free to ask for help, and gratefully receive it. And your life experiences would sync up to reinforce that belief.

To release mental clutter, get curious about your beliefs. If you find you're looking through ego-colored glasses, try on a new soul-affirming belief, such as *the world is a friendly place*, or *I can trust life*, or *everything is connected*, or *helpers are everywhere*. See what happens when you walk through your day projecting that belief. Watch how life syncs up and gives you evidence of the belief. With practice, and our soul glasses on, the clutter of unhelpful beliefs releases its hold and life can come into harmony with who we really are.

Watch Your Mouth

The words we use and the stories we tell are clues to hidden mental clutter. For instance, you may frequently use words and phrases generated by your ego mind, such as "I have to," "I should," "You should," "I'm not sure," "That's so annoying," "I hate," "I'm afraid that," "I'm worried that," "The problem is," "Whatever," or even worse. In the space of mindful awareness, you can experiment with words and phrases that are in tune with your true nature, like "Yes," "Awesome," "I'm grateful for," "I love," "I appreciate," "I'm excited to," I'm confident that," "I'm delighted by," "I can," or "I trust." Take a minute here to feel into the energy of these examples. You'll notice they have a higher vibration and feel better. Use the magic of 10 percent to incorporate them into your life.

Pay attention also to the stories you tell. The ego mind beliefs we most identify with tend to become our story. If you observe closely, you'll find familiar themes lurking. Some common ones are: *I'm broke. I'm wounded. I have to prove myself. I'm a victim. I'm better than. I have to sacrifice myself for others. People always abandon me.* To clear this type of clutter, simply begin listening to your stories. In the space of awareness, ask yourself how the story you are telling in any given moment serves you. Pay attention to the answer. Maybe it gets you sympathy, or approval, from others. Maybe it helps you get what you want. Maybe it makes you feel superior or inferior to others. If you have difficulty identifying your own stories, listen for the stories of others. Observing our fellow ego minds tell their tall tales gives us insight into our own.

To release this form of mental clutter, practice telling stories that support your soul intention and soul nature. Add 10 percent more soul to your stories by including new themes, such as: *I'm whole. I'm a creator. I have plenty. I care for myself. I'm worthy as I am. I trust myself and my knowing.* Our words and stories keep us anchored in who we are, or who we're not. We get to choose. Practice speaking only that which springs from your soul, feels good, inspires you and your fellow human beings, and adds love to the world. As you do, mental clutter will release.

Trust Your Intuition

Most of us rely on the "fake news" of our ego mind as our primary source of information. Understandable. The ego is the loud and ever-present voice that demands attention after all. But the soul is **also** a source of information. It speaks in a lower volume and a different language than our ego mind. It communicates through intuition, sending subtle guidance via gut feelings, heart knowing, or images, words, and symbols in our mind's eye. Our soul whispers to us all the time, trying to guide us in the direction of our true nature. But our ego mind, desperate to remain our sole source of information, does its best to drown it out. To access our soul's intelligence, we have to listen underneath the static of our ego thoughts. The way to do this, as always, is to come present. Presence quiets the ego mind, which then gives our inner knowing the opportunity to emerge. That's why we often have an epiphany or get a clear sense of what to do when we're in the shower, or out jogging, or driving in the car, or gardening. In those moments of presence, our ego dissolves and our soul has the chance to take the mic and share its wisdom.

It's not always easy to embrace our intuition in the face of our ego mind, or the influence of others. For example, when you know something doesn't feel right, but do it anyway. When you succumb to what others want you to do, even if it's not best for you. When you live from your head rather than your heart. When you fall in line with the herd rather than follow your own path. Clutter arises when we devalue, ignore, doubt, or deny our intuition.

To free yourself, practice tuning into the clear-seeing, clear-hearing, clear-sensing, and clear-knowing of your soul. Consult with your inner wise self often, in matters large and small. *What food would nourish me right now? Where should I park? What does my body need? What's the best way to approach this person? What do I know to be true right now? What's a solution to this problem I'm facing? What choice will create peace within me? What action is the most loving to me and others? What lesson am I refusing to learn?*

When you get mindful and ask, an answer will rise up from within. It may come in the form of words or images. It may come as a feeling or a body sensation. It may come as a knowing in your bones. Your attention might be drawn to a symbol on a passing truck, or a sign on the side of the road, or a line in a song you're listening to, or something you see in nature. Somehow your soul will send the information you need in a way that will be clear to you. Trust what you perceive. And then follow your soul's guidance, even when your ego mind, and other ego minds, try to convince you otherwise. Practice, practice, practice. With the certainty of our intuition at the wheel, we're on the road to freedom.

Summary

Ego-based thinking is part of us, but not all of who we are. To release the mental clutter of the ego mind, practice coming present whenever you can. Enter the space of mindful awareness where you have the opportunity for choice. Notice when you're in resistance and soften into acceptance instead. Use the magic of 10 percent to shift into thoughts, beliefs, words, and stories that affirm your true nature. Listen for the clear guidance of your intuition. As you anchor in the right mind of your soul, rather than in your ego mind, mental clutter and other associated clutter loosens its grip. This is the way of mental decluttering.

If you're interested in working more deeply with mental clutter and mental freedom, see the back section in this book titled Resources and Further Readings for two fabulous teachers of mind, and favorite people of mine, Byron Katie and Andy Shaw.

EIGHT

EMOTIONAL CLUTTER

*To be empowered—to be free, to be unlimited, to be creative, to be genius,
to be divine—that is who you are ... Once you feel this way, memo-
rize this feeling; remember this feeling. This is who you really are.*
—Joe Dispenza

Ego thoughts contain some version of *I am not enough, you are not enough, and
there is not enough,* and keep us bouncing between past and future time. When
we attach to these thoughts, we experience emotions such as sadness, shame,
guilt, anger, resentment, jealousy, insecurity, worry, anxiety, or fear. Put simply, we suffer. Ego-based emotions are emotional clutter, because they're not
in alignment with the natural emotions of our soul: joy, happiness, love, contentment, peace, and gratitude.

As I wrote this book, I came face-to-face with all kinds of emotional clutter, courtesy of my ego mind. I felt ashamed that I couldn't just get it done. I
resented that I "had to" write, rather than be out enjoying myself. My frustration hit new levels as I pored over the text, making change after change. I got
annoyed with friends who abandoned me in my writing struggles—for instance,
they didn't encircle me as I toiled, fanning me and feeding me grapes :). I worried that my choice to spend time writing, instead of working, would have dire
financial consequences. And I felt hopeless, certain it would all be a waste of
time. When we're hypnotized by ego-based emotions, we are out of contact with
present time and our soul nature. Rather than coasting along the open road of
positive and helpful emotions, we hit speed bump after speed bump.

Most of us are unaware of how ego-based emotions drive our lives.
We think these emotions are who we are. We assume that because we're

experiencing them, they must be true. We get accustomed to how they feel; uncomfortable as hell, but familiar. We unconsciously become addicted to the brain chemicals they pump into our system; craving adrenaline and cortisol like our morning triple shot venti soy latte with a caramel drizzle. The good news is there's another emotional reality, based in our inherent soul nature of peace, harmony, safety, and acceptance. Remember, the ego is part of our human experience, but it's not all of who we are. We can invite our soul to take the wheel and travel a new road.

To release the emotional suffering of the ego mind and shift into the emotional freedom of the soul, rely on and practice presence, mindfulness, resonance, and inspired action. Hold up whatever you find in your emotional closet to the light of the questions: *Does this emotion contribute to my soul intention? Is it beautiful? Is it useful? Does it love me back? Is it in present time? Does it have a sacred place to live? Does it help me serve my love to the world?*

Be the Witness

Emotional reactions are simply that, reactions to our thoughts. That's why coming present and witnessing our thoughts is the first step in releasing emotional clutter. As the witness, we can identify an ego thought we are attaching to that is creating distress. Chances are it isn't true, and it isn't in present time. Noticing and questioning a thought is often enough to release the attachment to it and return to emotional equilibrium. But if you find yourself mired in ego-based emotion and unable to detach from a thought, fear not. Continue to rely on mindfulness. Become the witness of your emotions. Have the experience (your emotions) and notice the experience at the same time, without judgment. As the witness, you realize one aspect of you is experiencing a difficult emotion, like anger or sadness or disappointment. And another, bigger aspect of yourself is not.

Whatever emotion shows up in a given moment is the one most in need of our love and attention. It holds the information we need to be more free. That's why the key to emotional decluttering is to welcome every emotion that comes to the door, and invite it in. Most of us don't even want to answer the door. We're frightened by the intensity of our emotions. We judge ourselves for having them. We fight to keep them at bay. We analyze them rather than feel them. We worry they will spin us out of control. We're afraid to be vulnerable, even with the people we love. We're convinced if we start crying, we'll never stop.

These are common tricks of the ego that keep us disconnected from the natural flow of letting go. The truth is, if you welcome an emotion and invite it in, it will stay for a while and then take its leave. Emotion is *energy in motion*, simply passing through. We've all witnessed this in children. A child can be hysterical one moment, wailing and inconsolable, and then suddenly calm again, face soft and sweet as an angel, happily eating an apple slice. Emotions move through children quickly and completely, exactly as they are meant to. We are wise to follow their lead.

Here's a way to be with your emotions mindfully. First, when an emotion arrives, welcome it, acknowledge it, and give it permission to be. Think of it like coming across an upset child crying on the curb. What would you do in that situation? Turn and walk away? Yell at the child to stop crying? Show the child how to push down the feeling? Start doing jumping jacks to distract the child? Well your ego mind might, but your soul self would never! You would sit down and gently ask what's going on. This is how to be with your own emotions; present, accepting, and willing to stay with them.

First, ask yourself "what's going on inside me right now?" and wait for the answer. This helps identify the emotion. Once you know what it is, say it out loud, just like the child on the curb would. "I'm scared ... I'm sad ... I want to go home ... I miss my brother ... she was mean to me." Then ask yourself "where is this feeling located in my body?" Your attention may be drawn to your constricted throat, nervous belly, tense shoulders, or that elephant sitting on your chest. This is valuable information from your soul about where you're holding onto unhelpful emotion, and where you can soften and release.

As you sit mindfully with an emotion, you may notice your body wants to do something. Maybe it wants to curl up in a ball, or make a sound, or rock, or shake, or sob, or simply shed a couple of tears. Let your body do what it wants. This is the emotion passing through. As you stay with the emotion and your body's response, ask yourself "when have I felt this way before?" You may see images from different times in your life, or one particular memory. This is information from your soul, linking you to an emotional thread of your life that's ready to be liberated. Trust this link and ask yourself "what is this image telling me about my soul's desires?" Your soul self will be so thrilled that you're asking, it will offer intuitive guidance such as words, an image, or a body sensation that lets you know where it wants to go. Here's an example from a client.

Mark and I were humming along, decluttering his closet. He had recently separated from his partner. He came across an old blue sweater on the shelf, and suddenly got quiet. I asked him "What's up?" and he quickly said "Nothing" and started digging in his sock drawer. Something was clearly going on. Since all of us adults have a child inside, I knew I had to meet him on the curb.

I asked him to sit on the floor with me for a minute. I said, "Can you tell me what you're feeling?" He shrugged and said, "It's no big deal, I'm good" but his jaw was clenched and he was pressing his lips together. I sat there quietly. Suddenly his eyes filled with tears, his upper lip trembled, and he blurted out: "I miss Kevin." Then he looked away and said, "Oh my god, I feel so stupid. I mean it's been almost three months. I shouldn't feel like this." I stayed right there, watching him try to push the feeling away by analyzing it.

Then I asked him where the feeling was in his body. He got quiet and then answered "In my stomach. It's like a giant hole in there. It aches." I suggested he put his hand on his stomach and just hold it there. After a minute or two he said, "That helps a little, like it's not so alone." Then his eyes filled up again. I asked him "What does your body want to do?"

"I just want to curl up right here but I think I need to get up and keep working."

He was in a key moment, the one where we have a choice to stay with an emotion or try to blow past it. I encouraged him to follow his body's request. He hesitated, then slowly rounded his shoulders, dropped his head, pulled his knees up to his chest, and within a few seconds was crying hard—a deep, heaving, man cry. The kind that feels like it has waited years to be released. I sat without saying anything, so as not to interrupt the energy moving through. After a few minutes, he stopped crying and his breathing slowed. Head still down, he said, "Whoa, where did that come from?"

I asked if he could remember a time when he felt this way before. He thought for a minute and said, "Hmm, that's weird. I just flashed to when my first boyfriend walked out the door and I never heard from him again. I couldn't believe he could walk away like that, like I meant nothing."

Here was information from Mark's inner wise self about an emotional thread of his life. I asked him, "What do you think this memory is here to tell you? What does it want you to know right now?" He stayed quiet for a bit and then, "I just got this feeling in my stomach, like warm and soothing. It's saying it's different now. I matter to me." Then he looked up: "Kevin gave me that sweater when we first got together. And when I picked it up, I just felt this moment of . . . like 'he left me at the altar.' Like the other guy. But it's not true. I know it's better for both of us to move on. It's gonna be okay. And we're gonna be kind to each other. And I'm gonna be kind to myself."

His eyes were clear and he was back in emotional equilibrium. Staying with the emotion helped him release feelings of loss in the moment. It also allowed an old relationship story to let go of him, so he could be in present time with how his soul wanted to move forward in relationship.

Being with emotions in this way takes practice, but it keeps ego-based emotions from accumulating in your inner cupboards. As you allow an emotion to come up and out, its energy releases, and your body relaxes. Good-for-you brain chemicals like dopamine and serotonin start to flow. A sense of calm and peace washes over you, indicating you are officially out of the clutches of your ego mind and back in touch with your true nature. You may even find yourself eating an apple slice.

Recognize Where You Hang Out

We all have emotional places where we hang out. For instance, you may be a person who spends a lot of time in emotions such as sadness, anxiety, or resentment. Even if these emotions are extremely uncomfortable, or downright toxic to your being, they are at least familiar. They somehow feel like home. But here's the thing: where we hang out emotionally matters.

Remember, ego-based emotions carry low vibrations which sync us up with matching vibrations in the world. For example, if you hang out in jealousy, you'll walk through the world comparing yourself to everyone, feeling better than one moment and less than the next. You'll see other people's good fortune and feel the injustice of your perceived lack. You'll have friendships with other jealous people, and your time together will be spent gossiping, second-guessing other people's choices, and finding creative ways to tear them down. If you hang out in shame, you'll walk through the world with your head down, trying your best not to be seen and feeling ignored or excluded at the same time. You'll avoid trying new things for fear of not being good enough. You'll be in relationships with people who diminish you or put you down.

In contrast, when you hang out in the expansive, higher vibration emotions of your true nature, life syncs up with you there. For example, if you hang out in joy, you'll walk through the world feeling upbeat and confident of your place in the world. You'll be generous with compliments; free to inspire others from your own deep well of inspiration. People will be drawn to your "good energy" and make an effort to spend time with you or bring you into new opportunities. Life experiences sync up to our emotions and the energy they carry, for better or for worse. In the space of mindful awareness, we can choose to hang out in emotions that sync us up with what we want for our lives and create less clutter.

Now if you're a person who hangs out far away from your emotions, you're in another type of clutter zone. For example, do you set your emotions aside to be dealt with later? Do you suppress your emotions, or try to rise above them with spiritual platitudes like *God never gives me more than I can handle*? Do you walk around feeling dead inside, safe from negative emotion but unable to access positive emotion either? Do you reject or deny certain emotions by showing up as the funny guy with your sadness buried within, for example, or putting your compassion on ice to get by in your corporate job?

When we cut ourselves off from an emotion, we lose access to the energy of that emotion. This is true for higher vibration emotions **and** lower vibration emotions. For example, in its pure form, anger carries the energy of destruction and re-creation; of taking action to change something. If you refuse to engage with anger, you can't harness this energy to deconstruct what isn't working in your life and create something new. In its pure form, loneliness carries the energy of belonging. If you refuse to experience loneliness, you can't harness this energy to find soul-affirming connection in your life. When you observe closely, you'll see how the emotions you avoid hold something of your soul nature. For instance, you wouldn't feel the emotion of guilt if you didn't love others enough to want to do right by them. You wouldn't feel betrayed if you didn't long for honesty and harmony.

If you've put an emotion in exile, a trip to your emotional storage unit is in order. You must bring the emotion home and give it a sacred place to live. To move freely through life as emotionally intelligent beings, we have to be willing to experience our full range of emotions, human and divine. With practice and mindful awareness, we can accept and honor all our emotions, and consciously choose where we want to hang out.

Shift Your Emotional State

As the witness, we're in position to recognize ego-based emotions and shift into emotions that are more of a match to who we are and that help us share our love with the world. It can seem like an impossibly long journey from stress to peace, sadness to joy, or frustration to contentment. But even a slight shift in emotion is significant, because it puts us one step closer to our natural state. Rely on the magic of 10 percent to gently shift your state and move up the vibrational scale. One way is to come present using your body. For example, if you find yourself in emotional turmoil, experiment with deep breathing. Draw your breath into your belly, or deeper into your pelvis, or even deeper into your feet. This keeps your attention focused on your body rather than imaginary places in your mind. If you breathe this way five or ten times, you'll notice your emotions start to settle down, thus changing your vibration.

You can also shift your emotional state by actively moving your body. Consult with your inner wise self about what kind of movement is called for. It might suggest turning on some music and dancing spontaneously, letting your body lead the way. It might recommend some gentle stretching or a leisurely walk to discharge an unhelpful emotion. It might propose pumping some iron or a vigorous bike ride. Coming present in our bodies releases emotional clutter and brings us to equilibrium, and the possibility of higher vibration emotions.

Another way to shift out of ego-based emotion is to come present using your mind. Remember, emotions stem from our thoughts. Emotions such as frustration, sadness, annoyance, fear, or rage often indicate resistant thoughts. If you feel these emotions, get curious about what you may be resisting. It may be something that's happening in a given moment (e.g., "I can't believe he just said that") or something that happened previously (e.g., "How could she have betrayed me like that?") or the emotional state you are currently in (e.g., "I'm so mad at myself for being so upset"). Resistance is like swimming upstream. When we drop into acceptance by acknowledging resistance and giving the emotion room to breathe, we float downstream into a different emotion and vibration.

If you find yourself emotionally activated, you can also use your mind in another way. You can choose to take a few minutes to distract yourself (i.e., bring yourself into presence!) by focusing your thoughts elsewhere. Do something you enjoy, like sewing or reading or cooking or walking your dog. Put on some music and let your attention be captured by the beat, or the melody, or the words. Engaging your mind wholeheartedly in something of the soul allows unhelpful thoughts and emotions to quiet down and release, leaving you in a different emotional state. To be clear, bringing yourself to presence is **not** avoidance; it's purposefully taking a break to allow emotions to loosen their grip and get you back in your right mind.

Respond Rather Than React

In the space of mindful awareness, we have the opportunity to respond, rather than react, to our emotions. Here's an example most of us can relate to.

You're driving on the freeway, and someone cuts you off. Suddenly you find yourself speeding by the other driver like a maniac, banging the steering wheel, yelling obscenities, and flipping him off. You go from zero to sixty in your thoughts, emotions, and actions. You react, meeting the situation with your ego mind. "Well, of course I did," you say. "That bastard could have killed me!"

There is another way. When we commit to awareness, as the witness, things slow down. Space is created between our thoughts, our emotional reactions, and the actions we take. So you're driving on the freeway and someone cuts you off. As the witness, you notice the thought "Jeez, he could have killed me." You feel your heart pumping and your hands shaking. You stay with the fear for a minute and reassure yourself that you're safe. The situation can end right there.

But even if you miss that part of your experience and find yourself enraged, that's okay too. You still have an opportunity to come present and observe. You can watch your anger and your ego mind's desire to retaliate. In the space of choice, you can choose not to take an impulsive action. Instead, you can take a big breath. You can shake out the tension in your shoulders and hands. You can continue driving the speed limit. You can mentally thank the other driver for reminding you to drive carefully. You can send him wishes for his safety.

Responding rather than reacting is emotionally intelligent and creates less clutter in our lives. Celebrate when your emotions truly get the best of you; the presence of your right mind and actions which reflect your true nature.

Keep Your Emotional Clutter to Yourself

When we're unwilling to deal with our emotions responsibly, or don't know how, we end up creating emotional clutter for others. One way we do this is by discharging our emotions on others, without awareness of their impact. For example, do you use emotional weapons like blame, rage, guilt, or shutting down to deal with your feelings? If your weapon of choice is rage, you might get annoyed by everything not to your liking, or lash out unpredictably, or have full-on emotional meltdowns. This keeps the people in your life walking on eggshells, unable to express themselves freely. If your weapon of choice is shutting down, you may refuse to talk about certain things, or express certain emotions. This leaves others confused about how to be in connection with you. Emotional weapons do not have a sacred place to live in your inner space or your relationships, so lay down your arms!

Another way we clutter others is by expecting or demanding others meet us where we are emotionally. For example, if you hang out in fear, you might say things that instill worry or doubt in others, such as "be careful," or "are you sure you want to do that?" This is you injecting your fear into their space, creating clutter for them. If you hang out in loneliness, you might expect people to be there for you whenever you need them. You might desperately seek contact or create extra emotional drama to make sure others show up for you. If you are angry in a moment, you might get outraged at anyone who won't join you there. As you stay mindful of your tendencies, you can practice connecting to others in a way that honors your true nature and doesn't burden them.

Avoiding our emotions can also clutter others. For example, you might get overly involved in your child's life to distract from the real issue; the despair you feel about your failing marriage. You might be unwilling to acknowledge a particular emotion, like anxiety, leaving someone else in the family to feel it for you. When we avoid our emotions, a big box of our emotional clutter inadvertently winds up in someone else's space.

A more subtle way we clutter others is by reinforcing their ego-based emotions, rather than their soul nature. For example, you may have a friend who is perpetually in emotional distress. You pride yourself on being there for her; supporting her side in the stories she tells and offering her helpful advice. This seems like a good thing, but you may actually be cluttering her. Your emotional need to be needed might unintentionally hold her in her false self. Taking care of your own emotions frees you to show up for others with true support, the kind that allows their soul's wisdom to come forth and show them the way.

If you see yourself in any of these examples, be compassionate. As you witness your impact on others, you'll naturally decide some containment is in order so you can share your love, rather than your clutter, with the people in your life.

Move Through Grief and Loss

When we're faced with loss from a breakup, divorce, or death, our ego mind goes into overdrive. We experience wild emotional swings; profoundly sad one moment and raging the next. We find ourselves living in memories of the past, or terror about what lies ahead. We're often unwilling to accept the person is no longer with us. We shut down emotionally because the pain seems too much to bear. Or, we get lost in swirling ego-based emotions, sometimes for months or even years. These are common responses to grief and loss that are part of our humanity. They soften in their own perfect timing, but we can ease our journey by remembering our divine aspect, which is also along for the ride. Grief, after all, is the price we pay for love.

Our soul nature is eternal, ever-connected, and not bound by the illusion of separation. Here are some ways to invite your soul into the driver's seat as you grieve:

Do your best to come present when you can. Welcome all your emotions. Surrender into acceptance of what is. Put everything the person taught you on paper, and in a sacred place in your heart, so it can guide your way. Trust that whatever happened was supposed to happen, and is in service to your path, whether it's clear to you now or not. Know that grief is love with nowhere to go, so look for places to share your love to honor yourself, the other person, and life itself.

Honoring our divinity, as well as our humanity, keeps us from accumulating emotional clutter. In the company of our soul selves, we can gracefully find our way after a loss.

Re-Think Trauma

When we experience a traumatic event, we often lose contact with our soul nature. There we are, rolling along in life, and then something happens that makes us question our safety, our intuition, the wisdom of trusting and connecting with others, or even the meaning of our existence. In the face of any kind of trauma, the ego mind kicks into high gear with some common responses. For example, our body and energy contract against life. Our emotions become frozen in time. We find ourselves in fear, staying vigilant so nothing like that ever happens again. We replay the situation over and over, convincing ourselves we were at fault for what happened and can never trust ourselves or other people again. We take on the identity of a damaged, inherently bad, or broken person. We become invested in either hiding this part of our personal story or leading from it. Traumatized quickly turns into hypnotized, courtesy of the ego mind.

When dealing with trauma, we have an important choice. Ego mind or soul mind? Choose carefully. Experiment with this soul-affirming approach.

Go back to the time before the traumatic event. See yourself living your true nature; trusting, loving, and engaging with life. This is where your healing lies. Trauma is an **attempted** robbery of the spirit, rather than a true robbery. *Our innermost being can never be tainted or taken from us, by anyone or anything.* Regardless of our human experiences, love is what we are made of and what we are born to do.

If you can consider this perspective, emotional clutter from trauma will begin to release. There will be more space for the soul truth that what happens to you, always happens for you. For example, you can acknowledge the resources you developed from what you endured. You can feel into the compassion you have for others as a result of your suffering. You can recognize the courage it took to travel such difficult terrain. You can rest in the knowing that because of your traumatic experience, you're especially equipped to love the world. This gives trauma a sacred place to live.

In mindful awareness, we can stay present to our soul nature as we deal with trauma, rather than abandoning ourselves, others, or the world. This frees us up to seek all the support we need to heal our body, mind, and spirit over time.

Summary

Ego-based emotions are part of us, but not all of who we are. To release emotional clutter, practice coming present whenever you can. Welcome all of your emotions with curiosity and compassion. Pay attention to where you hang out emotionally. Use the magic of 10 percent to shift into emotional states that help you serve your love to the world. Bring home any exiled emotions. Commit to respond rather than react. Take responsibility for your emotions, rather than cluttering others. Approach grief, loss, and traumatic experiences from a soul perspective. As you take inspired action, emotional clutter lets go of you. This is the way of emotional decluttering.

If you're interested in working more deeply with emotional clutter and emotional freedom, I've included information in the Resources and Further Reading section about Hakomi Body-Centered Psychotherapy, a mindfulness-based approach to emotional healing developed by the late, great Ron Kurtz, and expanded upon by the tremendous Jon Eisman.

NINE

ENERGETIC CLUTTER

*Don't ask yourself what the world needs. Ask yourself what makes you come alive
and then go do that. Because what the world needs is people who have come alive.*
—*Howard Thurman*

Everything is made of energy. We are energy, and we exist in a field of energy.
Energy flows within us, between us, in our environments, and in the world
around us. Low vibration energies such as lethargy, urgency, overwhelm, agitation, fear, dissatisfaction, needing, and wanting are the stuff of the false
self. Although familiar, they aren't the whole truth of who we are. They are
clutter in and of themselves and create other kinds of clutter. In contrast,
higher vibration energies such as vitality, inspiration, acceptance, enthusiasm,
confidence, and gratitude are the natural state of our soul.

We don't have to judge different vibrations, but we do need to be aware of
them. Vibe-ing in ego energy syncs us up with ego-affirming things. Vibe-ing
in soul energy syncs us up with soul-affirming things. In addition, ego and
soul energies we encounter in the world impact our vibration for better or for
worse. This is the truth of resonance. For example, even a walk down the street
can be a completely different experience based on the energy we're inhabiting.
In a low vibration moment, honking cars are irritating, the sidewalk looks
filthy, there are no friendly faces in sight, and you just want to get where you're
going. In a high vibration moment, honking cars are a background symphony,
the flowers poking up through the cracks in the sidewalk strike you as a
miracle, every passerby offers a smile, and you're content to be where you are.

As I wrote this book, I encountered all kinds of energetic clutter. My
energy often felt heavy and dull, like I was moving through sludge. I was

impatient about completing each new draft. I pushed myself to keep going even when I needed a break. I got overwhelmed by other people's advice and suggestions, as if they penetrated me and confused my own knowing. I rode an energetic rollercoaster, buoyed one moment by encouraging vibes from others, and defeated the next by discouraging vibes that also came my way. And throughout the long haul of writing, I dumped a boatload of low vibrations on my friends and family. (Sorry guys.)

Many of us travel through life at the mercy of ego energy, creating our lives by default. For example, maybe you feel agitated or chaotic a lot of the time, and just assume that's your natural energy. Maybe you allow ego energies of others to intrude into your space, leaving you feeling exhausted, sad, anxious, or angry. Perhaps you clutter others with your own ego energies of pushing, needing, or fearing. Maybe you live in a rhythm that doesn't suit you, rushing through your days at a frenetic pace, or dragging along waiting for something to happen. The good news is there's another energetic reality, based in our inherent soul nature of vitality, peace, contentment, joy, and love. Remember, the ego is part of our human experience, but it's not all of who we are. We can invite our soul to take the wheel and travel a new road.

To release the energetic clutter of the ego mind and shift into the energetic freedom of the soul, rely on and practice presence, mindfulness, resonance, and inspired action. Hold up whatever you find in your energetic closet to the light of the questions and look for yes answers: *Yes, this energy contributes to my soul intention. Yes, it is beautiful. Yes, it is useful. Yes, it loves me back. Yes, it is in present time. Yes, it has a sacred place to live. Yes, it helps me serve my love to the world.*

Be the Witness

To declutter our energetic space, it's essential to stay tuned to our soul vibration. This requires moment to moment awareness, because our energy is constantly in flux. It changes based on our thoughts, our emotional state, our habits, and our physical health. In addition, our energy is impacted by things outside of us, such as other people's energy or the stuff in our physical environment. To tune into vibration, take the position of the witness. As the witness, you have an experience (energy) and notice that experience at the same time, with curiosity rather than judgment.

There are several things to observe; your thoughts and emotions, your habits, your interactions with people, and your physical environment. The key is to pay attention to how they make you **feel**. The way you feel lets you know if you're in the vicinity of a vibration that supports your soul intention and helps you share your love with the world. Look for feelings of contentment, peace, aliveness, joy, enthusiasm, and love. For example, if a thought or emotion inspires you, it's a match to your natural vibration. If a green smoothie makes you feel energized, it's aligned with what your body needs. If you feel fabulous after spending time with a particular friend, he or she vibes with your soul. If a physical object truly makes your heart happy, it has a place in your life.

As you witness, also pay attention to what feels heavy in your life, and what feels light. Many people are living with a lot of weight; the weight of heavy hearts, relationship conflicts, extra pounds on their bodies, and too many possessions. Many people are living in darkness; the darkness of fear, violence, separation, and shame. Lightness and brightness are clues that something resonates with your true nature and is therefore worthy of a sacred place to live in your life.

In the space of mindful awareness, we have choice. We can choose to keep our energy high so we can sync up with things of a similar vibration. We can actively look for higher vibrations in the world to sync with. We can surround ourselves with things that feel good and amplify our vitality. Life changes when we get control of our vibration. Clutter releases and we come into harmony with vibrations that love us back.

Ground Yourself

Being in our best energy starts with being grounded; firmly planted, like an old oak with deep roots. When we're not grounded, we experience anxiety, insecurity, difficulty focusing, and disconnection. As one client described it: "When I'm not grounded, I feel scattered and unsure. It's like I'm here, but not here, and I can't feel my feet on the ground." In ungrounded moments, we're literally uprooted from the presence, solidity, and knowing of our soul self.

The easiest way to get grounded is to go outside. Even though we're all souls living in human bodies here on Mother Earth, most of us are not in consistent connection with her. We live mostly indoors, avoiding the elements. We wear shoes with rubber soles. We choose the sounds of television over the sounds of nature. We hunker down in the house at night, instead of being with the moon and stars. We purchase food rather than grow it. We can spend days without even touching the ground. Meanwhile nature is standing by, a free of charge, ever-present source of grounding.

When we spend time with nature, be it a forest or a single tree planted along the sidewalk of a major city, our energy naturally aligns with the earth's soul-affirming energy. Think of it like a baby. When a baby is in distress, the caregiver instinctively holds the infant against his or her chest. This soothes the baby, because their heartbeat syncs up with the caregiver's heartbeat. Just like a baby, we can sync up to the heartbeat, or frequency, of Mother Earth. Experiment with this and you'll see.

If you feel discombobulated, go outside. If you're hijacked by your ego mind, go outside. If you feel sick or fatigued, go outside. If you feel the energy of others intruding in your space, go outside. Sit or lie down on the ground if you can, and take your shoes off if you dare. Without you having to do anything, your body will begin to sync up with the earth's vibration. Your thoughts and emotions will settle down and the energy they carry will release. Your physical energy will be restored. Like the baby, you'll feel more relaxed, calm, and secure.

If you can't get outside, you can still connect with Mama Earth by looking out the window or immersing yourself in a picture of nature or in a nature video. Simply sensing the frequency of nature in these ways will help you ground. Try it out. See if you feel a little more peaceful, relaxed, and clear-headed when you allow nature in.

If you can't go outside or see outside, go inside! Visualizing nature is another effective way to ground. Here are some ways to do it:

- *Imagine yourself in one of your favorite natural settings.*
- *Visualize yourself as a tree with roots coming down from your hips and legs, deep and wide into the earth.*
- *Imagine yourself standing inside a mountain, solid and strong.*

- *Visualize yourself lying on the warm sand of a beach or floating in the ocean or a lake.*
- *Mentally place your whole body deep into the core of the earth, safe and held.*

Grounding helps us release energetic clutter and maintain a higher vibration. Practice these techniques often and stay mindful of your experience. Notice how your whole being quiets down. Watch how your belly softens and your breathing slows. How your shoulders drop, so you're no longer wearing them as earrings. Perceive how your body feels heavier, as if it's closer to the earth. Notice how you feel more present and on purpose. These are the telltale signs of being grounded.

Own Your Bubble

We all have an energy field around us, known as the aura. You can picture your aura as a bubble of energy that surrounds you, about a foot in all directions—front, back, right, left, above, and even below into the earth. Think of this lovely bubble as your protective cocoon. It belongs solely to you and is your energetic home. It is filled with energy that is generated by you and unique to you.

Let's take a moment to get to know your personal energy. Imagine yourself inside your bubble. Feel it all around you, like you are standing safe and protected inside a giant egg. Then ask your intuition to show you the *color* that represents your best energy. What color do you see? What is its specific shade? Is it bright or muted? Trust the information you receive. Next, ask to be shown the *rhythm* of your best energy. Hear it and feel it—is it like a soft pulse or a drum beat? Is it fast or slow? Smooth or staccato? Deep and strong or light and airy? Again, trust whatever information you receive.

The color and rhythm you perceive is your signature energy. Now imagine this color and rhythm flowing throughout your body and outward to the edges of your bubble. Feel yourself filled with your signature color, pulsing to your signature beat. This energy is yours alone and distinct from all other energies. It is your best energy.

Knowing your signature energy helps identify energetic clutter. If you don't feel your energetic best, you can come present and intuitively explore what's going on in your bubble. You might see a color that isn't your signature color or sense a rhythm that's different than yours. You might notice an emotion that's affecting your energy, or a particular part of your body that needs attention, or someone else's energy in your space. If any of these appear to you, some decluttering is in order. Here's an example.

My client Michael and I were working together in his garage. He seemed a bit agitated, moving through things quickly and being short with me, which wasn't his usual demeanor. I sat him down for a minute so we could explore what was going on energetically. He closed his eyes and took a few deep breaths to come present.

I asked him to feel into his bubble and his signature energy, which is a navy blue color with a steady kettle drum beat. Then I said, "Ask to be shown any energy in your bubble that isn't your best energy." He sat quietly, observing his inner experience, and responded, "I see the color red around my heart area." Staying with it, he then noted: "It's like it's making my energy faster than it wants to be." I inquired if there was any emotion connected to the red color and different rhythm. After a few seconds he said, "It feels angry ... and sad." I intuitively went one step further and asked if he could sense anyone else's energy in his bubble. He quickly responded, "An image of my sister just flashed in front of me." Then he made the big reveal: "We had a big fight last night and she hung up on me and I'm not sure what to do to fix it." A few seconds later he opened his eyes and said, "I forgot to tell you."

We both laughed, knowing that his agitated energy was the messenger. Through mindfulness, he recognized how energy from the interaction with his sister was still lodged in his bubble. The next step was to release it so he could come back to equilibrium.

Here are some fun ways to release energetic clutter from your bubble.

- *Imagine your bubble with a shower head at the top and a drain at the bottom. Visualize water coming out of the shower head, taking energy that isn't yours out of your body and your bubble and down the drain into the earth.*

- *Picture a white light coming down from the top of your bubble, illuminating energy that isn't your natural vibration, and beaming it into the earth.*
- *Imagine yourself with a hand vacuum, sucking up energy that isn't yours from your body and your bubble.*
- *Visualize a giant French coffee press going through your bubble, gently dislodging any unwanted energy to the ground (this one is Michael's favorite!)*

As you release unhelpful energy, imagine refilling your body and bubble with your signature color and rhythm until you feel back in your best energy. This is how to own your energetic space, release clutter, and keep your vibration strong.

Give Back and Reclaim

Energy is constantly being exchanged, for better or for worse. Most of us are unaware of the for worse part. We unwittingly welcome other people's energy into our space. For example, we try to connect with them by feeling their pain. We merge our energy bubble with theirs (picture the interlocking Olympic rings) to really be there for them. We take on their pace or energetic needs to the detriment of our own. When you allow yourself to be an energetic dumping ground for other people, your energy field starts to resemble the Peanuts character Pigpen.

Stay curious about how you allow your energy to be compromised. For example, observe how your energy changes as you get caught up in someone else's mini drama, such as their frantic search for their wallet or their missing car keys. Notice what happens to your energy when you get overly involved in someone else's financial problems or relationship crisis. Watch how you inadvertently let another person's anxious, depressed, or angry energy become yours.

As the witness, look for the unmistakable signs you've allowed your bubble to be breached. Your mood might change, leaving you sad, irritable, or drained. Physical symptoms like nausea or a headache may come on unexpectedly. You might feel energetically attacked, like you've been kicked in the gut. You might feel trapped in a conversation or a situation. You might start to feel confused about something you were clear about before. You might find yourself in an ongoing mental conversation with someone after your interaction has ended, unable to get them or their problem out of your head.

If you don't feel like your best vibrational self after an interaction, it's time for some energetic decluttering. Other people's energy doesn't love you back and doesn't have a sacred place to live in your bubble. To release it, come present and scan your bubble to find where the energy of the other person landed. Once you find it, you can give it back. It's just like if you found something in your office drawer that belonged to someone else. You would remove it and return it, because it's not yours.

When you declutter your bubble, you give energy back mentally, using your imagination. First, acknowledge you've found someone else's energy in your heart, or your stomach, or the back of your bubble, or underneath your feet. Then apologize in your mind for accepting it because it belongs to them and they need it. And then mentally send it back, out of your bubble and back to theirs. Once you release it, you can cleanse your bubble with a shower of white light to re-establish your energy as yours alone.

As you practice this technique, you might notice energy in your bubble that you let in a long time ago. For instance, you might be holding onto the energy of betrayal from a past relationship. You might carry the energy of someone else's rage or fear, convinced it's yours. You might have energy from a traumatic experience stuck in your bubble. It takes presence and awareness to keep your bubble just for you. With practice, you'll get better at giving back what doesn't belong to you and keeping your bubble wholly yours and in present time.

Now to the reclaiming part of energy exchange. Just like you, other people have their own energy bubble, and their own signature energy. When you allow **your** energy to extend like octopus tentacles into someone else's bubble, that makes YOU energetic clutter in their space. Get curious about your energetic impact. Do you dump your problems on others? Do you rely on other people to keep you grounded or lift your spirits? Do you expect other people to live in your rhythm? Do you try to fix or change people? Do you devote too much of your energy to someone else's life? If any of these are true for you, have compassion for yourself. In the space of mindful awareness, you can choose to be more energetically responsible so the people you love can be free to live their own best energy.

After you interact with another person, practice reclaiming your energy. Mentally retrieve it from their space and bring it back into your bubble. As you do so, apologize mentally for your interference in their energetic business. Your energy doesn't love them back and doesn't have a sacred space to live in their bubble. As you practice this technique, you may realize you've left some of your energy behind in other times and places. For example, your energy may be in a project you never finished, or a failed relationship, or an unfulfilled dream. It may be in a physical location where you once lived, or in a difficult experience. If you ask, your inner wise self will show you exactly where to find your energy. Wherever it is, you must mentally go get it and bring it back home, because it doesn't belong there. It belongs with you.

If you notice any resistance to giving back or reclaiming energy, observe it with love. Like all clutter, energetic clutter serves a purpose. Here's an example.

Chloe had gone through a brutal divorce seven years prior. As we were decluttering a file cabinet in the basement, she came across a thick file wedged in the back. It held a paper record of the divorce; copies of nasty email exchanges between her and her ex, fear-inspiring letters written in lawyerese, and psychological evaluations required in the custody battle. She said, "Oh, I definitely need to keep that," set it on the floor and continued on.

A few minutes later she remarked how seeing the file was triggering. So I asked her to take a moment to see where the divorce was still wedged in her energy field. In mindful awareness, she said, "Well I can see there is still a lot there." Then she put her hands on her upper chest and said, "It's like he's still here in my throat area, pushing my voice down." She started to cry, and said, "The divorce was so horrible, and I had to watch every word I said for so long."

*I asked how it would feel to send his energy back to him. She started to laugh through her tears and said, "But I would feel lonely without it. I'm just so used to it even though it feels like shit." This little nugget illustrates how the ego holds onto fear and the familiar. Then I asked her to tell me about the energy she left in **his** energy field. She smiled and said immediately,*

"Oh, I left my dream of family there. And anger for how he screwed me finan-cially. I still remind him every chance I get." Then she had this insight: "I didn't want him to move on too easily with his new wife and forget about me."

We spent some time mentally sending back his energy and retrieving hers. As we did, her energy got stronger, as if she was being restored. She began to spontaneously hum, as if the stuck energy in her throat was leaving and her voice was returning. After a while, she said, "I know we're connected forever, and we really loved each other. I just want to live my life and let him have his."

There it was ... the truth of her soul, wise and graceful. It hung in the air for a minute, and then Chloe opened her eyes, went to the shredder, and began releasing the papers she knew she didn't need to keep anymore. Releasing the energetic clutter she thought she couldn't do without allowed physical clutter to let go of her. As we know, it's all connected.

P.S. The next day Chloe and her ex had their most civil parenting exchange in years, reinforcing the magic of decluttering.

When we give back and reclaim energy, everybody wins. We all need to be in possession of our own energy to gracefully walk our soul's path. As we anchor in our soul selves, and fall in love with our personal energy, it becomes natural to treat our bubble, and every bubble we meet, with respect and reverence.

Shift Your Energetic State

When we become observers of energy, we start to recognize the vibrations that love us back, and the ones that don't. In the space of awareness, we're free to shift out of low vibration energy and into soul-affirming energy using the magic of 10 percent. One way to do this is to come present in your body. Ground yourself or do some deep breathing. Make some slight adjustments in your body; smile, relax your hands (notice how this releases your jaw), lay down and let yourself melt into the floor or the earth, or stand tall and raise your arms in a victory pose. Even these small changes will affect how you feel.

You can also shift your energetic state by actively moving your body. Do some impromptu dance moves. Shake out your head, neck, shoulders, arms, and legs. Get your blood pumping with a brisk walk or a few pushups. Movement brings us to the present moment, gets energy flowing, and raises our vibration. Consult with your inner wise self about what would be helpful. Don't be surprised if it suggests stillness, or a few minutes in child's pose, or a nap. Rest is often exactly what's needed to change our energetic state for the better.

We can also use our thoughts to shift our energetic state. Remember, energy flows where attention goes, so what we think about matters. Putting your attention on helpful thoughts will help raise your vibration. One way to do this is to find a reason to feel good in any situation. For example, if you're stuck in traffic and feeling frustrated, look for something you can appreciate. It might be the wildflowers on the side of the road, or the fact that you even have a car to drive, or the kindness of the driver in the next lane who just let another car pass.

Another way to shift your state is to find the best thought you can in any given moment. In the space of mindful awareness, ask yourself, "what thought can I focus on right now that's better than the one I am thinking?" For example, if you're obsessing about getting laid off at work (ego thought), shift your attention to a thought that is more true in present time, such as *I am employed right now, and if that changes I will deal with it then.* If you're thinking about how awful it is that you don't have the new iPhone 77 (ego thought), shift your attention to something you do have, such as *I'm grateful I have enough money to pay my rent this month.*

When we put our attention on the best thought we can find, unhelpful energy lets go of us and we feel better. And as we know, the better we feel, the better our vibration. And the better our vibration, the better we feel. With presence and practice, we can ease into vibrations that truly love us back, because they sync us up with more of what we want in our lives. Also, when we locate in soul energies (e.g., aliveness, peace, acceptance, and gratitude), lower vibration energies in the world that aren't a match don't have a place to sync. They'll follow the law of resonance and either rise up to meet us or seek an energetic match elsewhere.

Shhh...

Noise is an ever-present type of energetic clutter. Noise comes from within, in the form of thoughts and emotions that aren't true to our nature. It comes from outside, such as the sounds of leaf blowers, thumping car stereos, and the nonstop chatter of other ego minds. It comes as information overload: 24-hour news, endless podcasts and magazines, intrusive advertising, and ego-affirming social media. And it comes in the form of habits that dull our aliveness and presence, such as eating junk food, abusing substances, or staying constantly busy.

The ego mind relies on noise to keep us distracted from our soul selves. It convinces us the noise is the stuff that really matters. It convinces us the noise is the truth, and the only way to belong is to engage with it. Most people mindlessly consume all the noise. Maybe you are one of them. It looks like this: You're Facebook friends with everyone and keep up with several news feeds throughout the day. You're currently watching three different series on Netflix. You have a pile of books on the bedside table you're certain you'll get to someday. You talk on your speakerphone in public. You rely a little too much on wine and chocolate. And you have a serious case of FOMO—Fear Of Missing Out.

To declutter the noise in your life, become the witness of its energy. For example, get curious if your thoughts and emotions lift you up or drag you down. Pay attention to how the sounds in your environment impact you. Watch how your body responds to those four cups of coffee or late-night cookie binges. Notice how the daily news about politics and the economy and crime makes you feel. Observe what happens to your energy as you binge watch two seasons of a show written by ego minds for other ego minds to devour.

As you stay mindful, energetic clutter will reveal itself. If it takes you away from presence, it's clutter. If it creates fear of any kind, it's clutter. If it keeps you in the trance of not enough, it's clutter. If it makes you feel dull, agitated, or dissatisfied, it's clutter. If it creates pressure to keep up, it's clutter. If it lowers your vibration, it's clutter.

Most of us spend the majority of our time tuned into noise, leaving little space for the quiet of our inner world. But in all spiritual traditions, there is a call to enter silence. In silence, our minds and bodies settle down and our energy is restored. We reconnect with ourselves. We get to enjoy things we usually miss, such as birds chirping, leaves rustling, or the delicious sound of silence itself. We gain access to our own information and intuitive messages that move us along on our path. Being in silence is a radical act. Try it right now. Just sit quietly for five minutes. Observe your experience without judgment. It may be challenging at first. Your thoughts might get active, or you might feel anxious. If you stick with it, and comfort your ego mind, any initial discomfort will subside.

To release the energetic clutter of noise and add more quiet, use the magic of 10 percent. Turn off the TV. Drive to the store without the radio on. Put your phone in timeout for an hour. Take a short vacation from social media. Say no to any more articles about how to parent your children or better your sex life or succeed at life like a celebrity or become a millionaire. Change your morning alarm to a soothing sound. Go hiking without your headphones. Eat and drink things that calm your system. Be with nature for a few minutes each day. Try one morning a week in silence or get really radical and try a whole day (carry a small notepad to answer questions from the kids!). With practice, you'll get better at discerning what is noise for you and what feeds your soul.

You can also practice engaging with the incessant noise of life in soul-affirming ways. For example, see if you can find a quiet place inside, even when there are jackhammers pounding in the street or in your own mind. Subscribe only to magazines that contribute to your soul intention. Let the sound of your text message notification be a cue to go inside, take a deep breath, and come present. Surrender into any noise you can't control, like that car alarm going off next door or the siren screaming by, rather than brace against it. Watch the news from inside your energy bubble. In the space of mindfulness, we can remain undisturbed in the noise and poised in our soul energy and serenity; knowing if it costs us peace, it's too expensive.

Come into Balance

Every human being contains masculine and feminine energies. Masculine energy is the energy of will and action, doing and focusing, planning and controlling. Feminine energy is the energy of creativity and emotion, imagining and dreaming, receiving and surrendering. When these energies are out of balance, we experience energetic clutter that cascades into other forms of clutter.

When our masculine energy is in overdrive, we find ourselves in constant action, overworking and overdoing. We feel a sense of pushing and urgency. We dominate others. We're self-critical. We live from our head, rather than our heart. We achieve, but don't enjoy the process. In contrast, when our masculine energy is diminished, we have difficulty bringing projects to completion. We're passive rather than active. We lack the discipline and confidence to do what we want to do in the world.

When our feminine energy is in overdrive, we have difficulty regulating and containing our emotions. We give up our authority to others. We're full of ideas but unable to take action. We struggle to integrate the intuitive information we receive into our lives. In contrast, when our feminine energy is diminished, we find ourselves out of rhythm with our natural cycles. We doubt our intuition and our soul longings. We mistrust life. We feel out of contact with the broader spiritual fabric.

In mindful awareness, we can embrace our masculine and feminine energies and actively draw from each. For example, if you notice you're relying too much on masculine energy, make space for 10 percent more feminine energy. Slow down and tune in. Create something, such as a piece of art, a poem, or a beautiful meal. Find ways to laugh and play. Delegate household chores. Nurture your body with acupuncture, restorative yoga, dance, or time in nature. Enroll in a class about matters of the spirit. Change up your daily routine. Look for magic.

If you're relying too much on feminine energy, make space for 10 percent more masculine energy. Start a project and complete it from beginning to end. Engage in your choice of physical activity to bolster your strength. Exert your will to complete tasks around the house that you've ignored. Enroll in a class that stimulates your analytical mind. Do something for yourself rather than for someone else. Assert your knowing. With our masculine and feminine energies in balance, we're better able to live our soul intention and serve our love to the world.

Summary

Freedom from energetic clutter becomes possible when we recognize that vibration matters. To release energetic clutter, pay attention to the energy of everything in your life. Stay mindful of low and high vibrations, so you can consciously sync with helpful energies. Look for what feels good, light, and bright. Stay grounded, ensconced in your bubble and signature energy. Honor your energetic space, and the energetic space of others. Stay mindful of your energetic state. Explore the noise in your life and embrace the quiet. Find the balance in your masculine and feminine energies so you can express all of who you are in the world. As we become more energetically responsible, our experience of life changes from the inside out and the outside in. This is the way of energetic decluttering.

If you're interested in working more deeply with energetic clutter and energetic freedom, I've included information in the Resources and Further Reading section about two master teachers and dear friends of mine. Francesca McCartney introduced me to many of the energy skills in this chapter, which are just the tip of a beautiful iceberg of material she offers in her book and online school. James Van Praagh is a world-renowned spiritual medium who has written many bestselling books and also teaches life-changing energy skills through his online school.

TEN

RELATIONSHIP CLUTTER

My first impulse now is to always find something to love, something to be inspired by, something heroic, something recognizable as the gift and burden of the human condition, the pain and grace that's there to find in every soul you meet.
—*Ron Kurtz*

Relationship decluttering is an invitation to look at all of our relationships and the ways we relate within them. In this chapter we'll explore our relationship with our physical body, ourselves, other people, money, nature, and the unseen realms. The quality of our relationships is determined by who is in the driver's seat. When the ego is at the wheel, blasting "Not Enough" on the radio, we relate from a place of fear, lack, and separation. For example, if conflict, competition, disrespect, or power struggles are the norm in your relationships, your ego likely has a tight grip on the wheel. When you fail to treat another human as the <u>being</u> they are, your ego has hijacked a relationship moment. Allowing the ego to drive our relationships creates clutter.

In contrast, when the soul is at the wheel, the cool sounds of "Enough is Enough" keep us relating from a place of safety, acceptance and connection in present time. This keeps our relationships clutter-free. If your relationships are characterized by harmony, interdependence, gratitude, and compassion, your soul is at the wheel. When you treat another being with kindness, acceptance, and neutrality, your soul is present for a relationship moment. Becoming soul aware in our relationships gives us the freedom to engage in new ways.

While writing this book, I came face-to-face with clutter in all my relationships. I got in the habit of drinking coffee to face the shit-show of getting my thoughts in order, but it gave me heart palpitations that dishonored my body. I discovered layers of low confidence and unworthiness in my relationship with myself. My tendency to focus on other people's needs didn't jive with the laser focus and alone time writing demanded. I commandeered relationship moments with endless talk of my process, burdening my friends and reinforcing the ego lie of not being enough. I re-evaluated certain relationships when it became clear they were not in alignment with my soul intention of completing this book. I moved in and out of fear about my finances. And I often forgot to rely on nature and unseen support to stay calm and write on.

Take a moment to explore how relationship clutter shows up in your life. For example, do your daily habits negatively affect your health or well-being? Do you question your worth or abilities? Are you a fixer? Do you stay in relationships that don't honor who you are? Do you put the needs of others ahead of your own self-care? Are you in ongoing conflicts with family members, your boss, or a particular friend? Do you dim your light around certain people? Are you in constant fear about money? Do you fail to see your connection to all things, seen and unseen? The good news is there's another relationship reality, based in our inherent soul nature of peace, acceptance, harmony, love, collaboration, and connection. Remember, the ego is part of our human experience, but it's not all of who we are. We can invite our soul to take the wheel and travel a new road.

To move from the relationship clutter of your ego mind to the relationship freedom of your soul, rely on and practice presence, mindfulness, resonance, and inspired action. Hold up whatever you find in your relationship closet to the light of the questions: *Does this relationship or way of relating contribute to my soul intention? Is it beautiful? Is it useful? Does it love me back? Is it in present time? Does it have a sacred place to live? Does it help me serve my love to the world?*

Be the Witness

To free ourselves from relationship clutter, we have to become the witness of our relationships and our ways of relating in any given moment. As the witness, we have an experience (relating) while noticing that experience at the same time with curiosity and compassion. We're grateful for anything we notice, as it's a signpost on the road to freedom.

First, pay attention to your feelings as you engage in the different relationships in your life. Notice when you feel anxious, ashamed, resentful, or angry; and when you feel peaceful, accepting, loving or neutral. Pay attention to body sensations that accompany your feelings, such as a tightening in your chest, a sick feeling in your stomach, a rush of sweetness and joy, or the softening of safety. Feelings are clues to whether a relationship or way of relating supports our soul intention and loves us back.

Second, pay attention to energy. Notice when you connect with others in energies such as worry, urgency, competition, and complaints; and when you connect in acceptance, harmony, playfulness, and enthusiasm. Pay attention to energetic clues like discomfort or ease, constriction or expansion, and deflation or inspiration to know whether a relationship or way of relating is useful to you.

Third, observe resistance. When things don't go the way our ego wants them to, we resist. We say a big no to whatever is happening. We get angry, or start a fight, or just walk around the kitchen muttering, stubbornly holding onto our position. Most relationship issues stem from resistance, so look for relationship moments when you can surrender and be with what is. Yes, my wife just let the dog out and the gate is open. Yes, my colleague lied to me. Yes, my son left without mowing the lawn. In the space of mindful awareness, you can accept what is, even if you want something different. You can choose to stay dedicated to your peace of mind, respond rather than react, and embrace harmony over disharmony.

Fourth, become an expert witness of how you relate ego to ego, rather than soul to soul. Here's an example we've all experienced.

You're having a pleasant conversation with your friend, and then she gets triggered by something you say and starts to argue with you. You forget this means she's temporarily asleep, with ego at the wheel, and your own ego jumps into the fray, arguing back. Now there are two people out of their right minds.

The argument escalates until she shuts down with a righteous "Whatever." You trump her with a "Fine, whatever" and walk away. It doesn't stop there. Now you're replaying the argument in your head, or telling another friend about it, keeping the ego energy alive. Recognize this kind of ego-relating?

Here is the soul-relating alternative. Your friend starts to argue with you. You know immediately her ego is at the wheel. You remain calm and neutral, rather than taking it personally and being sucked into an ego battle. You hold the energy of acceptance and compassion for her distress. You acknowledge her perspective or ask a question to shift the energy back to harmony. If she still wants to argue, you lovingly say, "I don't want to participate in an argument." And then you honor your soul nature by releasing the interaction there, instead of carrying it into the next moment in your own head or dumping the energy of it on someone else.

As you focus on relationship clutter, you'll have many opportunities to observe how you relate from your ego and from your soul. Just watch. This will put you in a position to choose how you want to engage. Now let's take a look at our various relationships to see where the ego might be in the driver's seat, and where the soul can take the wheel.

Relating to Your Physical Body

Our physical body is our soul's home. It's the one possession we have to keep for our entire life, yet we don't always treat it with the reverence it deserves. Do you ignore your body's need for sleep, water, or exercise? Do you ingest food that's devoid of life? Do you chronically pump your body full of stress hormones? Do you overindulge in alcohol, caffeine, or other substances? Do you judge your body relentlessly?

Get curious about the clutter in your soul's home. Stay present and observe, even if it's difficult to watch. The ego mind is the mind that makes these dishonoring choices. Over time, these choices become habits that are often in conflict with our soul desires. For example, you might long to know who you are, but your habit of drinking alcohol keeps you from the presence and self-reflection needed to find out. You might want to take better care of yourself, but your habit of staying up late playing video games keeps you from having enough time in the morning to exercise. You might desire more even-keeled emotions, but your habit of bingeing on sugar keeps your moods unstable.

The good news is that a habit is simply a habit. Just like we developed the helpful habit of brushing our teeth every day, we can create any habit we want. In the space of mindful awareness, our soul gets a chance to weigh in. It might offer up a new habit, such as spending a few minutes a day in nature, or drinking a large glass of water before each meal, or greeting your body each morning with a loving affirmation. It might reveal a way to serve the purpose of an existing habit in a soul-affirming way. For example, maybe you can wind down at night by doing something creative rather than watching that crime show. Or perhaps the energy you find in your coffee cup might just as easily be found in some morning yoga poses.

Remember, the ego's job is to keep us doing what is familiar, so go slowly. Use the magic of 10 percent to relate to your body in new ways. Add 10 percent more of what makes your body feel good, loved, nourished, and cherished. Release 10 percent of what doesn't. As you do so, unhelpful habits will begin to let go of you.

It's important to note that habits sometime solidify into full-blown addictions. All addictions are attempts to contact things of our soul nature, such as relaxation, aliveness, expansiveness, balance, vulnerability, creativity, or connection. The impulse toward the divine self is there, but the pathway is misguided. If you're cluttered by addiction, please seek the help you need to meet your true nature with true presence and self-loving actions.

Our physical body can also reveal our hidden clutter and soul longings, if we're willing to ask. In the space of mindful awareness, we can communicate with our body to access its wisdom about what is ready for release, and what wants to emerge. Here's one way to do it. Come present and mentally scan your body from head to toe. Look for the place that is saying "Pay attention to me!" Once you find it, ask what it wants you to know right now. For example, if your attention is drawn to the extra body weight around your middle, ask how it serves you. If you notice tension in your shoulders, ask what it needs. If your attention is drawn to the pain in your hip, converse with the pain so you can understand its purpose at this time in your life. If you suffer from heart palpitations, inquire about the message they're trying to convey. If you have an ongoing health condition, ask how it wants you to grow. Very often, physical symptoms are soul dreams trying to come true. Here's an example from a client.

Jen had suffered a broken leg. She was laid up in bed, struggling to accept her situation. She was mad at her body for failing her. It seemed like a good time to help her relate to her body differently. So I invited her to write a letter from her injured leg to herself, to find out what it wanted her to know at this time. She thought I was crazy (what else is new?) but agreed to do it. The letter surprised her. Her leg told her she needed more time in stillness, and less time in the work drama that had been consuming her. It wanted her to put her attention on a dream that had been percolating inside: to create a website to help women navigate the perils of divorce. Communicating with her body in a new way created space for a soul longing to be heard. All she had to do was ask.

Relating to Your Self

Our relationship with ourselves is our primary relationship. This inner encounter is the foundation for all of our other relationships. When we recognize ourselves as souls in human bodies, this relationship immediately changes for the better. We feel our inherent worth. We know we're necessary and that we belong, no matter the job we have, the number of cars in our driveway, the color of our skin, our sexual identity, or our perceived failures. We stand firm in the soul truth that we are here for one purpose, to share our love with the world. Get curious if any of the following kinds of clutter are present in your relationship with yourself. Practice the strategies offered to relate to yourself as the being you are.

Cluttered souls struggle with self-love.

If you observe closely, you might notice that many of your everyday thoughts, feelings and actions don't reflect a heart that loves itself. For example, do you criticize yourself harshly? Do you disregard your own needs? Do you look for others to give you what you want, and end up disappointed when they don't? Self-love is not a big, lofty thing. It happens in a moment. To love yourself better, focus on what you can give to yourself. Take a rest when you feel tired. Eat some carrots instead of carrot cake. Think a kind thought about yourself. Say what you want to say instead of what you think someone else wants to hear. Put your dirty clothes in the hamper rather than on the floor. Take a few minutes to do something for yourself before you tend to someone else. These are all radical acts of self-love. They build your self-love muscles and get you in shape to love more freely.

Cluttered souls don't trust themselves.

Do you have difficulty making decisions, or question the decisions you do make ad nauseum? Do you frequently consult others for their opinions or advice, instead of trusting what you know is best for you?

Become an expert witness of how you don't trust yourself. When you observe yourself saying things like "I'm confused," or "I'm not sure," or "I don't know," or "What do you think?" drop in a little deeper. Ask your soul self: "Assuming I do know, what's the answer?" With practice, you'll begin to access your inner wisdom and learn to trust it. If you find you're afraid to make a mistake, or spend a lot of energy lamenting decisions you've already made, consider this soul-affirming perspective. There are no mistakes in life, because everything, without exception, is in service to your soul's growth. Review your life thus far to see how this is true for you. From there you're free to relax into a new level of self-trust and release some significant clutter in your relationship with yourself.

Cluttered souls don't honor their preferences.

If you pay attention, you might notice you habitually do what others want you to do, rather than what you want to do. You might realize you're not even present with yourself to know your own preferences. In the space of awareness, you can recognize and choose what feels good and right to you in any given moment, knowing it will love you back. For example, you might prefer to read a book instead of yak on the phone. You might prefer to eat at a healthy breakfast place rather than at the greasy spoon your friend is suggesting. You might want to go for a leisurely jog, not a hard-core run, with your exercise partner. You might prefer to sit outside and watch the rainstorm even though your husband wants to keep watching TV inside. We often worry we'll be abandoned by others if we assert our preferences. Ironically, we end up abandoning ourselves.

Relating to Others

In relationships, we shift endlessly between our ego and soul minds. That's why you can love your wife in the morning and be calling a divorce lawyer in the afternoon. While we're moving in and out of our right minds, so is everyone else. That's what makes relationships so challenging, so beautiful, and so susceptible to clutter. Let's be very clear. Letting go of relationship clutter is not about tossing people out like old pairs of shoes. It's about determining 1) if our relationships are in alignment with our soul intention, and 2) if our ways of relating in any given moment are based in ego or soul consciousness.

First, we have to be curious about whether our relationships are in present time and support our soul intention. A relationship might be based in past time, in that it once made sense but doesn't fit who you are now. It might be based in future time, such as if you're waiting for someone to change so you can have the relationship you want. It may no longer inspire you or feed your soul, because it doesn't support all of who you are and what matters to you most. It may not have a sacred place to live, for example if you're having an affair or hiding a relationship from your loved ones.

As you declutter, you might decide to put an ego-affirming relationship on the back burner or bring a soul-affirming relationship back to life. You might even decide to move on from a relationship because it's the most honoring thing to do for you and the other person. Remember this. If a relationship isn't beautiful to you in present time, it doesn't make the other person bad or wrong. It simply means the relationship isn't your soul's preference at this time in your life. It's kind of like being at a salad bar. If you love olives, you put some on your plate. If you're not a fan of olives, you don't stand in line judging them: "Oh, I can't stand olives ... that drab green color ... that intense salty flavor ... that dangerous pit." You simply don't choose them. It's the same with people. Rather than condemning those you don't resonate with as "toxic" or "screwed up" or "bad," think of them as a preference or not, like an olive. It's neutral, not charged. It's kinder. It allows everyone to move freely in and out of relationships. If a relationship is ready to let go of you, release it lovingly, without holding the other person out of your heart. Be grateful for the time spent together, trusting you will both find your way to new relationships that serve your souls' growth.

Secondly, we have to stay mindful of how we relate from ego and soul consciousness. The ego keeps us in our false selves, relating to the false selves of others. It constantly looks for things it doesn't like in others and convinces us we're *not like that*. If it sees something of our true nature in others, it convinces us we're *not like that* either. The truth is, we're all kindred spirits, moving in and out of our human and divine aspects and treating each other accordingly.

Relationship decluttering is an invitation to remember who we really are and act from it. As you observe how you relate, you'll get better at spotting who is at the wheel in any given moment. You'll see how most of your relationship issues have more to do with your ego than with anyone else. In the space of awareness, you can choose to show up in your kindest, wisest, most understanding self in a relationship moment. In the clarity and grace of soul relating, we're prepared to be the love needed in any given moment, and to do the loving thing needed in any given moment. We're free to show up with a hug, give a compliment, take out the trash without a snarky comment, be generous, choose connection rather than ambition, ask "how can I help?," be inspired by someone else's energy, or accept someone else's way.

Be aware that decluttering can create temporary turbulence in your relationships, as the people in your life wonder what the hell is going on with you! As always, ride the waves, trusting that soul-relating is ultimately in service to you and everyone else. Get curious if any of the following kinds of clutter are present in your life. Practice the soul strategies offered and watch how your relationships change.

Cluttered souls look for love in all the wrong places.

Do you put the burden on others to *make* you feel loved? Do you compromise yourself to *get* love? Do you mistakenly believe you can *lose* love? Do you fail to realize that when you're lonely you are actually missing **your** (soul) **self**, not another person? Love is your natural state. It originates in you, belongs to you, and exists wholly within you. It's an inside job. Your responsibility is to come into presence, where your love can always be found. When we're sourced from the inside, rather than wanting or needing from others, we're in position to share our love rather than our clutter in our relationships.

Cluttered souls have difficulty receiving.

Do you reject compliments or gifts? Do you complain about the way someone shows their love and support? Are you constantly there for others, but unwilling to let them be there for you? These not good for the soul ways of relating are actually driven by our ego. Our soul is always willing to receive. It knows that receiving is a win-win, because as we receive we nourish ourselves **and** simultaneously allow others to nourish themselves through sharing their love. Stay present and watch how your ego mind says no to the flow of giving and receiving. Try a morning where you say a wholehearted yes, thank you! to everything that comes your way. It might be uncomfortable at first, but it will open your eyes to where you constrict against your nature. And it will put you in the vibe of gratitude, which is exactly where you want to be.

Cluttered souls see vulnerability as weakness.

Do you hide your mistakes or failures? Are your most tender feelings protected by a cache of emotional weapons? Do you try to conceal your humanness, such as your greed or your jealousy? The unwillingness to be vulnerable is actually ego fear disguised as strength. It creates all kinds of clutter, inside and out. To release this clutter, try a new way. Admit your fears. Say "I don't know." Tell the truth. Cry if something moves you. Acknowledge when you do something that hurts someone else. Show you care. Ask for help. Admit when you're wrong. Apologize. As you practice being vulnerable, you might be surprised. Vulnerability releases the false self, and paradoxically helps us feel stronger and more authentic. It also gives others permission to be more fully themselves with us. Win-win.

Cluttered souls are confused about boundaries.

Loose or rigid boundaries indicate that our ego is at the wheel. For example, maybe your boundaries are loose. Your clothes infringe on your husband's side of the closet, your judgmental thoughts hit people with not so nice energy, or you're afraid to say no to what someone else wants. Loose boundaries indicate we're willing to violate ourselves or others to get what we think we need. In contrast, maybe your boundaries are rigid. You have strict daily routines, refuse to consider new viewpoints, or have a wall around your heart that keeps others out—and you trapped inside. Rigid boundaries are a declaration of what we don't want or won't accept, think we need or demand to have. They are unyielding and keep us from dancing with life in the moment.

Soul-based boundaries stem from knowing who we are and honoring our preferences in the moment. They come from the deepest yes. They reflect that we feel safe and secure inside, able to meet our own needs. They respect other people's space, feelings, and choices. They implicitly honor the knowing and preferences of others. When we say "no" from a clear and kind place, and "yes" from a clear and kind place, and allow others to do the same, we're enacting soul boundaries. As you choose boundaries that honor yourself and others, clutter releases.

Cluttered souls fight for their false selves.

Do you rabidly defend your ego-based beliefs? Are you full of justifications for your unhealthy habits or addictions? Do you deny other people's intuition? Championing the false self is an act of violence against ourselves and others. To release this kind of clutter, take a few hours of your day and refuse to put up any defenses. If someone criticizes you, look for the nugget of truth in what they are saying. If someone shares their intuition, welcome it. If someone states a point of view different from your own, acknowledge their perspective and do your best to join them. Notice where you argue for your own limitations, or the limitations of others. And ask yourself often, do I want to be right or in relationship? Defending our false selves ties up energy. When we offer no defense, energy is liberated and, in that moment, we are free.

Also pay attention to how you use relationships to perpetuate your false self. For example, maybe you're *waiting* for your alcoholic partner to change, because you secretly fear you can't make it on your own, or you're *lying* to your brother about something you did so you don't have to risk his rejection. Perhaps you're *pretending* you don't pay taxes on time because the government is crooked, when the truth is you struggle to keep agreements. Maybe you're *hoping* your boss will acknowledge your efforts with a raise, because you're terrified to advocate for yourself. Perhaps you're *hiding* a truth about yourself from the people you love because you fear their judgment, and secretly judge yourself. Maybe you're *denying* the guilt you feel about the good things in your life, or *wanting* something other than what you have.

Many of us live in these "-ings" of the ego mind. They are among the subtle, and not so subtle ways we lead from our false selves. Our soul selves are interested in a different set of *"-ings"*—*loving, being, seeing, knowing, accepting, trusting, nurturing, flowing, creating, transforming, and truth-telling.* Practice living from them and watch clutter fall away.

Cluttered souls hold onto hurt.

We have all hurt other people, and we've all been hurt. The truth is, we can only hurt others if we are overidentified with our ego thoughts and emotions, and therefore out of contact with our soul nature. Even if we hurt someone "on purpose," we can still only do so if we've been hijacked by our ego mind. All hurts, even the intentional ones, are perpetrated by ego mind believers, asleep at the wheel and out of their right minds. And yet, we all hold onto the energies of pain, guilt, and regret for hurting another person, or the energies of anger, hate, or blame for being hurt. These energies keep us separate from our loving nature. The way to release this kind of relationship clutter is to understand *there is only ever one thing to forgive*: that we were out of our right mind or someone else was out of their right mind.

Holding this soul perspective keeps our hearts open. We're free to forgive ourselves for being asleep at the wheel and accept the consequences of our actions. We're free to forgive someone else for being asleep at the wheel, even if they hurt us in the deepest way, and let them experience their own consequences. We're free to remember what happened, and release the unhelpful energy connected to it. And we're free to choose if and how we want to be in relationship going forward. Forgiveness keeps us in present time, with love flowing and hurts healing.

Cluttered souls won't take responsibility.

Do you blame the so-called bad things in your life on others, or minimize your part in the good things in your life? The places where we won't take responsibility are clues that our ego is fighting to keep our false selves intact.

The bigger truth is that we create everything in our lives. Understanding this frees us to safely take responsibility for everything and create our lives in service to our soul.

To practice, take a day and accept responsibility. *Yes, I said that. Yes, I did that. Yes, I tried to manipulate you. Yes, that was really my fault, not yours. Yes, I blame you for my problems so I don't have to change. Yes, I tell the story that what you did to me caused all the suffering in my life.*

Take responsibility for the good too. *Yes, I was kind in that moment and uplifted someone else. Yes, I stayed in my energy bubble at work and the meeting went better. Yes, I worked hard to be good at what I do. Yes, I stayed calm during the getting ready for school chaos and the morning went smoothly. Yes, I shared my feelings and now my wife is sharing hers. Yes, I'm a talented writer.* As we take ownership, we come into alignment with our true nature and clutter releases.

Here's another way to take responsibility in your life. When you catch yourself pointing your finger at how other people relate, follow the clinched fingers pointing back at you all the way home to yourself. Here are some examples.

If you notice yourself complaining that your boss is ungrateful, get curious about where you are ungrateful. If you're frustrated that your wife won't be spontaneous, acknowledge where you fight for control. When you hear yourself telling the story of how your brother abandoned you, find the ways you abandoned him, or abandon yourself. If you're inspired by someone's peace or creativity or kindness, honor that capacity in yourself. We're all in this together, in a house of mirrors. And in a house of mirrors, all we can see is ourselves and our personal responsibility. In that clear reflection, we can also see our freedom.

Cluttered souls interfere.

Do you give unsolicited advice or judge how others live their lives? Do you try to solve problems that aren't yours to solve, or enable others to avoid the consequences of their actions? When we interfere in someone else's life, our ego is at the wheel, masquerading as our soul self. Interfering is a misguided attempt to save someone, without knowing their true salvation. It creates clutter and has unintended impact. Interfering sends a message to the other person that we don't trust them, or life itself. It implies they don't have the wisdom and resources to deal with life their way.

Observe how you presume to know what's best for someone else. Pay attention to how you get embroiled in things that really aren't any of your business or offer help that may not actually be helpful. To release this kind of relationship clutter, take a big step back and settle into your energy bubble. Commit to be with others with your presence, not your solutions. Speak to them in your soul voice, rather than in one that mirrors their ego mind; chastising, criticizing, fearing, doubting. Trust them to be their own authority and make their own decisions. Accept their choices. Trust life enough to know that whatever they do will ultimately contribute to their soul's growth. If you find you have advice to give, practice giving that advice to yourself, instead of them, and see if you can follow it. Staying in our own business, and letting others handle theirs, creates less clutter in our relationships. As we hold space for someone else's path in life, and support their soul nature and wisdom, we release ego-relating and enter soul relating.

Cluttered souls are conflicted in their social lives.

Do you make commitments you don't really want to make, and then create clutter by breaking them? Do you engage in social activities that no longer interest you? Do you spend too much time alone, when you long for connection? Do you schedule yourself down to the minute? Come present and observe your social life. Get curious if it is in harmony with your soul intention and truly loves you back.

If not, remember that small changes can make a big difference. Add 10 percent more space in your calendar to allow for spontaneity. Reduce the time you spend in stressful or draining social situations by 10 percent. Balance the scales of social stimulation and alone time. Spend 10 percent more time with people who don't want something *from* you but want something *for* you.

And here's a little soul to soul permission slip. Social engagements are times when we share our love. If you're not up for them, it's okay to decline. Your ego will try to convince you there will be major fallout if you don't attend the party or show up for the potluck. Rely on your deeper knowing that everyone will survive and may even be inspired by your choice. If you absolutely must attend a social event, but are resisting, see if you can drop into acceptance. When you stop struggling, you'll open yourself to the nugget of magic that will be there waiting for you.

Cluttered souls are in relationship agreements that no longer serve.

Relationships start with agreements that create bonding and harmony. When these agreements, or contracts, are made by ego minds, they are problematic. Some examples are: *I'll put your needs ahead of mine. I'll take care of you even if it means abandoning myself. I'll hide your addiction if you hide mine. I'll stay loyal to you by not being myself.* In contrast, relationship agreements made by souls allow both people to live their true nature. Some examples are: *We honor each other's needs, rhythms, and talents. We're self-loving individuals coming together to love each other and the world. We commit to come back to love when our ego minds collide. We can both have what we want.*

Get curious about your relationship agreements. If you chronically feel underappreciated, misunderstood, burdened, or even abused, it indicates a contract needs updating. If you can't bring a relationship contract into present time to support both of your souls, it may mean the contract is complete and your time together has reached a natural end. If so, trust it's okay to let go, and commit to create soul-affirming relationship agreements moving forward.

Relating to Money

Like every relationship, our relationship with money reflects who is in the driver's seat. When we relate to money primarily from our ego mind, we're convinced there's never enough and we always feel at risk. We constantly worry about making money or losing money. We feel insecure no matter how many zeroes are in our bank account. We hoard what money we do have, rather than using it to help others.

With the ego at the wheel of our financial life, our relationship with money is *out of present time.* For example, you might find yourself hanging out in past time, lamenting financial choices you once made or holding onto old shame about money. You might locate in future time, for example, worrying you won't have enough money to live on for the rest of your life or holding onto things you don't use for fear you won't have money to buy them again.

With the ego at the wheel, our money habits *don't love us back.* For example, you might spend impulsively to impress others, or feel unworthy of putting money towards your health and well-being. You might forget to pay yourself first by putting a little bit of what you earn into your savings before spending elsewhere. When the ego is at the wheel, our relationship with money *doesn't have a sacred place to live.* You might spend more than you earn or earn less than you're worth. You might be secretly in debt, or late on your taxes. You might judge others for their financial abundance, or their poverty. You might buy things you can't afford, or don't really need, to keep up with other ego minds. When the ego is driving our financial life, our focus on money gets in the way of us *serving our love to the world.* For example, you might stay in an unfulfilling job in the name of money or work so hard you get physically ill. You might pursue material possessions and achievements over things that matter to your soul, such as time with loved ones or creative pursuits. An ego orientation to money is a clutter game with no winner.

When our soul is at the wheel of our financial lives, we relate to money differently. We define ourselves by who we are, not what we have. We know we belong whether we have a hundred dollars in the bank or a billion. We live in present time, knowing there is enough and appreciating what we have. We take care of our financial responsibilities in an honest and timely manner. We recognize that the best things in life are free. We know money for what it is, simply one form of exchange in our society to take care of our needs. We realize we've always had exactly what we needed, even in the toughest of times. Your ego will balk at this, so spend time reviewing your financial history to see if it's true.

To create a more aligned financial life, begin with acceptance. Judging yourself won't change things. But getting honest and accepting what is will lead you out of fear and overwhelm and into inspired action. The first step is to clear the clutter in your money's home—your wallet! Chances are it's stuffed with faded receipts, crumpled bills, more credit cards than you need, and the hidden abundance of unused gift cards. Begin by treating what's in there with respect. And then introduce new financial habits using the magic of 10 percent. Come into 10 percent more financial integrity by taking care of what you owe before spending money on things that aren't essential. Spend 10 percent less each day and put the difference in your savings account each month. Add 10 percent more gratitude and appreciation for what you do have. Spend 10 percent more on soul-affirming expenses, like an art class, or better food, or helping others prosper. Find your most elegant balance among spending, saving, and sharing.

Staying mindful puts you in position to introduce some soul into your finances. Here's an example from a client.

Jasmine's soul intention was honesty and integrity in her life. As we sat in her office, she told me she was responsible for the family finances. At first glance, she appeared organized. She had categorized bills in a big binder. Her desk drawer held neatly arranged files. But then I noticed an overflowing basket of paperwork on the floor. When I asked about it, she said "Oh that's just pending stuff, bills I need to deal with." And then she dragged a plastic bin out from underneath the desk. "There's this too." It was filled with color-coded files. "Oh, and one in the garage."

As we dove in, it became clear that Jasmine was not on top of her finances at all. Like many people with clutter, the truth was masked by the appearance of organization.

It took several days to go through all the paperwork. As we sorted and released page by page, we discovered where her ego was at the wheel and her financial life was out of integrity. For example, we came across credit card statements that showed thousands of dollars of debt. When I asked her about them, she replied, "I don't like to think about what I owe because it freaks me out. I just pay the minimum every month."

Jasmine also revealed that she had taken money out of her retirement accounts to pay debts incurred by her husband, who was also in the red. She said, "He begged me to help him, but now I don't have a safety net." She described herself as an ATM for her teenage sons, afraid to deny them what they wanted. She realized that she rarely spent money on her own well-being. Her relationship with money kept her in constant stress and accruing more debt.

Jasmine knew it was time to stop procrastinating and avoiding, and start getting her financial house in order. We created a household budget and a plan for her pending bills. She set most of her accounts to paperless delivery to break the cycle of paper clutter. She contacted her credit card company for help and told her husband the financial enabling was over. She increased her work hours to full-time to significantly reduce her health insurance premiums. She shared the truth of the situation with her sons and they began spending time together differently, purchasing less and relating more. In a bit of decluttering magic, we found a pre-paid debit card tucked in one of her files and immediately applied it to a past due medical bill, setting the resonance to becoming financially free.

Jasmine knew it would take time to bring her financial life into alignment, but she was out of denial and in the momentum of inspired action; on the road to a more soul-based relationship with money.

True security comes from a solid connection to our soul, not legal tender. True abundance comes from sharing our resources and creative gifts in service to others, not extravagant consumerism. True financial freedom comes from being in right relationship with money. When we locate in these soul truths, we always have the right amount of money for us and receive what we need when we need it. Energy tied up in fear and worry is liberated and can be used to create more of what we want financially.

Relating to Nature

Our relationship with nature also reflects who is in the driver's seat of our lives. Do you ignore nature as you move through the day? Do you dominate nature by maniacally weed-whacking, or cutting down perfectly healthy trees because they make a mess in your yard? Do you endlessly order from Amazon, without concern for the ecological impact? Do you fail to acknowledge plant, animal, and tree beings as no less than human beings? These are examples of clutter in our relationship with nature.

Meanwhile, nature is standing by, ready to show us all we need to know about our true nature. If you put your soul glasses on, you'll see that everything in nature has a place and a role; nothing is more important than anything else, and everything is interconnected. You'll also see that everything in nature exists within us. For example, we're mostly comprised of water that is the same salinity as the ocean. We experience clear skies and cloudy days in our minds. Our emotions can stir up like waves or be as peaceful as a morning lake. We're expansive as the sky, and no less solid than the mountains. We have periods of dormancy and fertility, growing in natural cycles. We hold the deep wisdom of trees.

With your soul glasses on, you'll also notice that clutter doesn't exist in nature. Only what is essential is there. Dead things decompose, rather than collect in natural cupboards. Everything has a sacred place to live. A bush, a rock, an ant, a swamp, and an eagle are all necessary and important, exactly as they are and where they are. When a leaf is done with its purpose, it lets go and falls to the ground in perfect acceptance. The trees that share our world model connection, collaboration and "there is enough" by sharing nutrients through their roots so other trees can flourish.

Nature tells the truth. In mindful awareness, we can allow it to share its wisdom. When you're in nature, come present and take it in with all your senses. Look at things, touch things, smell things, and listen. If you have a particular question about your life, ask nature to show you an answer, and trust what you perceive. If you have any internal clutter you're ready to release, such as an outdated belief system or some unfinished business, let nature help. Find something in nature that represents what you're ready to release, and then leave it with a tree, or bury it in the ground, or offer it to the ocean. When we view nature from a soul perspective, we enter right relationship with the earth. We feel a duty to honor and protect nature, because to betray it is to betray our own true nature.

Relating to the Unseen Realms

The ego defines reality using our five senses. It will argue that if we can't see it, smell it, hear it, taste it, or touch it, it doesn't exist. This keeps us located in the material world, convinced that what we experience day to day is the ultimate reality. But the larger truth is that we're in this world but not of it; we're human beings born of a bigger, unseen reality.

We glimpse this oneness and connection in the present moment, when our ego momentarily dissolves. In presence, we transcend everyday consciousness and momentarily touch the unseen world. For example, we've all experienced things we can't explain with our ego minds. We whisper to our friends about them: "Wasn't that a strange coincidence?" or "It's such a small world, right?" or "That butterfly was a sign from my mom ... I just know it." Then our ego mind tries to convince us we're making it up. Even if we believe it deep down, we often hide it or make a point not to talk about it, when we should be shouting it from the rooftops.

With our souls at the wheel, we're free to experience the mysterious web of soul connection that holds us all. For example, take a moment right now to come present and think about a loved one who has passed. Your ego might have you convinced that they are gone and your relationship is over. But your inner wise self knows that their eternal spirit remains in your life. Imagine them sitting next to you, or in front of you, or behind you; as close and as real as anything else. Feel their presence, their energy. And then open the lines of communication. Spend some time talking with them in your thoughts or out loud. Write a letter to them or let them write a letter to you. Ask them for whatever you need; guidance, support, or a sign about your best way forward in life.

Souls don't die; they simply continue in a new form. If we embrace this soul knowing, we can maintain relationships with those who have left the body. We can relate to them in their new form, even as we miss them and long to feel them in the flesh. Here's an example from a client.

Heidi grew up as a child of divorce. When her dad left, her mom married an abusive man. Heidi was angry with her biological father for most of her life. She resented him for abandoning her and her mom. She was convinced he didn't know how to love. Heidi's father died when she was in her thirties, but her heart remained closed to him even now, in her fifties. On our last day of decluttering, my intuition told me we needed to go through the last drawer in the guest room dresser.

She opened the drawer and found a small white box wedged behind some light bulbs, battery packs, and extension cords. She took it out and began to look through it. Lo and behold, it was full of letters from her deceased father to her mother. These letters told a very different story about him; a story of love and commitment. It was extraordinary to watch Heidi get to know her father's soul as she read the letters aloud. She had longed for connection with him her whole life but couldn't get past the story that had dogged her since she was a child.

Now she was experiencing a different truth about him. There was no denying it. Her eyes got brighter as the burden of who she thought he was began to release. Now she had permission to love him. She decided in that moment to build her relationship with him in present time, in his current form as spirit. She began to think of him as her wingman in life, guiding her towards her soul longings.

She knew they both shared a love of nature, so she brought him along on her bike rides and walks through the woods. She asked for signs that he was with her, and they came in the form of heart-shaped rocks she found on the trails. She didn't let her ego mind dismiss these signs, but instead celebrated them by making trail markers and little altars to brighten the day of other people on the trails. Heidi's willingness to open herself to her father's ever-present love and support helped her release a bunch of relationship clutter. It also put her on a new path to studying shamanism and aligning her life with the deep connection and loving guidance of the spirit realm.

The departed walk with us unseen, yet alive in spirit. Relate to them this way and watch how life changes.

We live in a vibrant universe, with seen and unseen allies all around. Now that may sound a little freaky but stay with me. In addition to the people in our lives who have passed, there are also ancestors, nature spirits, angels, and spirit guides working within us and around us. They exist in a universal field of energy and information, present but unseen, working together for our greatest good. They are as real and reachable as the living human beings in our lives.

When we enter our soul knowing, we can feel them there, patiently waiting to show us the way. It's like having our own personal spirit team; partners in our true nature, walking with us on our soul's path. If you're open to it, learn about them. Be in gratitude for their presence. Build relationships with them so they can protect, heal and guide you. Ask for their support to help you stay grounded in your soul intention, and to embody your gifts. Relying on this web of support helps us navigate our lives as the eternal, connected souls we are.

Summary

Freedom from relationship clutter becomes possible when we're willing to stand in our soul nature and act from it moment by moment. To release relationship clutter, acknowledge the essential relationship between your soul and your physical body, and practice more intentional self-care. Identify yourself as a human being and drop into a new resonance of self-worth, self-confidence, and security. Enter right-minded relationship with yourself, others, and money. Choose relationships that nourish your soul in present time. Practice ways of relating that offer acceptance, peace, and harmony. Be aware of your impact on other beings and their impact on you. Be with nature to remember your true nature. Connect with the unseen beings who can help you on the road to a more soul-directed life. This is the way of relationship decluttering.

If you're interested in working more deeply with relationship clutter and relationship freedom, the teachers mentioned in previous chapters offer practical and inspiring guidance. I've also included information in the Resources and Further Reading section for Lucid Living, an in-depth coaching program developed by soul sisters Leza Danly and Jeanine Mancusi.

ELEVEN

PHYSICAL CLUTTER

The best things in life aren't things.
—Laurence J. Peter

My eighty-year old friend Jerry recently said to me, "Guess what Peggy? I'm downsizing ... to an urn!" His dark humor held a gorgeous kernel of truth. We are here temporarily. When we depart this planet, none of our stuff goes with us. And yet, we hold on tight to what we have and chronically acquire more. I don't have a lot of possessions, but as I wrote this book, physical clutter still reared its ugly head. For example, I shopped for things I didn't really need to distract myself from the arduous task of writing. I accumulated crystals and objects from nature to support my process, and they ended up crowding my space. At times, my bedroom looked like a clothes bomb went off, and I noticed my thinking was in similar disarray.

To find out how physical clutter shows up in your life, schedule a house tour with your soul self as your guide. Start at the front door and wind your way through every room, the basement, the attic, and the garage. Commit to seeing clearly. Your stuff may be scattered about in full view or hiding in turquoise bins in the office, vacuum-sealed bags under your bed, and fancy cabinets in the garage. If you really look, you'll be shocked by how many candles and sneakers and dishes and books and spice bottles and kitchen gadgets and t-shirts and computer cords and dog toys and skin care products live in your home.

You'll also realize you can survive a few years without buying pens, sticky notes, computer paper, staples, or sharpies for your office. You'll see you have enough lawn care products, sporting equipment, car wash supplies, and tools for the entire neighborhood. You'll recognize you have more stuff than one person or family could ever use. And you'll glimpse the irony that in your house full of things, in all that abundance, you feel a sense of too much but somehow not enough. The good news is there's another reality, based in our inherent soul nature of peace, contentment, sharing, and enough-ness. Remember, the ego is part of our human experience, but it's not all of who we are. We can invite our soul to take the wheel and travel a new road.

To free yourself from physical clutter, rely on and practice presence, mindfulness, resonance, and inspired action. Ask the questions about everything in your home. *Does it contribute to my soul intention? Is it beautiful? Is it useful? Does it love me back? Is it in present time? Does it have a sacred place to live? Does it help me serve my love to the world?* As you look for yes answers, the possessions that are not essential—not of your essence—will reveal themselves and begin to release, lightening your load.

Be the Witness

There are several things to witness as we sift through our stuff. First, pay careful attention to your state of mind. You want to feel good as you declutter. What's more fun than a release party after all?! Be on the lookout for signs of resistance, such as feeling overwhelmed, frustrated, unmotivated, forced, or avoidant. Remember, resistance is a glimpse of the ego fear that created the clutter in the first place. Be grateful when you notice it and anchor into your soul intention when you can. Go slowly and start with the stuff you feel least attached to so you can build confidence and gain momentum. If you are in any way hesitant to release something, don't. When it's truly time for it to let go of you, it will. Easily.

Second, observe where your environment is out of present time. If you're hanging out in *past time*, you'll notice a plethora of things that don't feel like you now, such as that Beatles poster from college, the formal living room set from your first marriage, or the leather pants from your clubbing days. You'll have an abundance of items from the past, like your adult son's Legos, the floppy disks from your graduate work, old leashes from dogs passed (RIP Fidos), or the paperwork from the house you sold ten years ago. You'll have functional things you don't use anymore, like the queen-sized sheets that don't fit your new king, unopened packs of file folders from your corporate days, or the racing bike in the garage.

If you're hanging out in *future time*, you'll have a lot of things you keep "just in case," such as the crutches from your knee surgery three years ago (just in case you have surgery again), the ancient printer in the office closet (just in case the new one breaks), the original box for the floor lamp in the basement (just in case you move), or the old treadmill in the garage (just in case your daughter wants it someday). You'll have things you don't use but refuse to get rid of because you "don't want to buy them again," like the fancy juicer in the bottom kitchen cupboard or the couture jacket in the back of your closet. You'll have extra of everything: legal pads, wine bottle openers, pillows, coffee mugs, suitcases, hangers, flashlights, saucepans, blankets, and those plastic shaker bottles with the wire balls in them. Decluttering is an invitation to bring ourselves and our environments into *present time* by keeping only the things we love, use, and truly need to live our current soul intention.

Third, observe the energy of your environment. Most people are so accustomed to their stuff, they don't even notice it. It's just there. And it's usually been there a long time, in exactly the same way. Sometimes I enter a home and it energetically feels like a haunted house: sepia-toned, with white sheets hanging over the furniture, and cobwebs everywhere. The energy of the space isn't in present time.

To get a feel for the energy you live in, take an energetic walk-through of your home. Imagine you're seeing it for the first time. Enter the front door with curious eyes and your spider sense tingling. Tune in and trust what you perceive. Sense the areas that feel weighed down, stagnant, or neglected. Notice the places that feel light, serene, clean or energizing. Imagine water flowing through the space to identify where clutter may be inhibiting energetic flow. (Hint: those boxes stacked in the corner of the guest room, that stuff on the floor under your desk, the comforters crammed onto the shelf in the linen closet, and the random items stored beneath your bed all obstruct flow). As you move through your space, acknowledge any energetic truths you've been denying, such as the dread you feel every time you pass the stuffed hall closet, or the way your heart sinks when you enter the garage, or how the random shoes strewn in the entryway make you a little crazy every day. Whether our clutter is out in the open or behind closed doors, it affects us energetically. Here's an example from a client to bring that point home.

> *I once worked with Brenda, a woman whose husband had died from cancer, leaving her a single parent to a 10-year old girl with autism. There was a converted garage in the house that was filled with stuff she hadn't touched in the four years since his death; the space was frozen in time. Brenda was ready to address it.*
>
> *We were cautious not to disturb any of her daughter's things, as she was very sensitive to change. We decluttered everything else in the room. We removed her husband's golf equipment, paintings, sweatshirts, and old papers. We released things of hers from their time together that she no longer needed. We cleaned out the random trash and the broken things that had found their way into this stagnant zone of the house. We put the remaining stuff neatly on the shelves. When Brenda's daughter got home from school, she walked in and looked around. We stood waiting, hoping she wouldn't become agitated by the dramatic change. After a long 20 seconds, she smiled and said, "Mama ... I can breathe."*
>
> *This is the energetic impact of releasing clutter and bringing a space into present time. Suddenly there's room to move, a rush of relief and lightness, energy available for new things, and space for new breath.*

Fourth, get curious about what your physical environments reflect about you. For example, the kitchen is a place of nourishment. Your fridge might be empty except for some old lettuce, a few beers, and a six-pack of soda. Your cupboards might be packed so full you don't even know what's in them. Expired food may live on your pantry shelves. What you observe in your kitchen can tell you something about how you nourish yourself.

The bathroom is meant to be an area of self-care. But your cabinets may be stuffed with old makeup, expensive products you never use, and medicine from five years ago. Your shower caddy might be loaded with half-used shampoos and shower gels you don't really like. Stained, bleached, or ripped towels may hang on your towel bar. What you observe in your bathroom can tell you something about how you care for yourself.

"Horizon-tal" surfaces reflect personal horizons, or a sense of the future. Your desk may be piled with papers to the point where you can't see the top. The windowsill might be lined with your glass dolphin collection, requiring contortions to open the window. Your shelves may be stacked precariously, as if they might topple at any moment. What you observe on your horizontal surfaces (don't forget the top of the refrigerator!) can tell you something about how you envision the future. Our physical environment is always speaking to us and about us. Listen to what it's saying.

Lastly, observe how each and every possession makes you feel. You're looking for the things that inspire happiness, enthusiasm, gratitude, and joy. When you hear yourself say "Oh, I LOVE that!" you're right where you want to be. That item vibes with your soul. You love it, and it loves you back. As you declutter, you'll find many things that just don't do it for you. They might feel neutral, or just so-so, or downright repelling. Celebrate when you find these things, as they are easy releases. Also, if you find you have multiples of something, like ski jackets, double down on how each one really makes you feel. If you're honest, you'll realize you only treasure one or two, and they are the ones worthy of prime real estate in the coat closet.

Keep Like Things Together

People who struggle with clutter tend to have stuff all over the place, rather than in one place. This leaves them feeling fragmented, rather than whole. For instance, you may have similar things living in different areas of your home. There are clothes in the bedroom closet and the guest room dresser and on the rack down in the basement. Light bulbs live in the office closet and the kitchen drawer and the dining room cupboard. Office files are in the desk drawer and the file cabinet in the bedroom and the banker's boxes in the garage. Art supplies can be found in the office and on the shelf in the den and inside the TV stand. As you declutter, bring like things together to live in the same place. It helps you feel less fragmented, and also makes you less likely to overbuy because you forgot what you have.

You might also notice you have dissimilar things living together in your home. For example, the basket on the kitchen counter holds coupons, old receipts, magazine articles, loose change, some photographs, a phone cord, and that paperwork you need to sign. The pile on the dining room table contains a few books, some gift cards from your birthday, a package you need to send, an uncashed check, your child's homework, and a single sock from the laundry. The guest room closet holds a random mix of things: memorabilia, old linens, unhung artwork, and some, but not all, of your tax files.

As you declutter, sort your things and create dedicated places for them. Photographs in the photo bin. Random cords and computer paraphernalia that you truly need in the technology drawer. Tax stuff on the tax shelf. Medical paperwork in the medical file. Loose change in the abundance jar. Sorting reduces chaos and fragmentation; there's a place for everything, and everything is in its place where you can find it easily. I drive my clients crazy by constantly asking "where will it live?" If there is no obvious answer, there may not be a place for the item in your life.

Some people take fragmentation to the next level by storing possessions outside their home. Your wedding gifts from five years ago are stashed at your parents' house. Your old skis and a crate of albums reside in your friend's garage. Your fraternity stuff from college is still in a box in your ex's basement. You pay money every month to keep "important" things locked up in a storage unit across town. If any of these are true for you, go and visit your stuff. Chances are a good portion of it can be released, because by the nature of where it's living, it's not essential. If you find things you want to keep, bring them home so you are all in one place.

Land the Plane

Cluttered souls tend to leave things undone. They have difficulty completing cycles of action or *landing the plane*. Do you let the mail pile up on the counter for days, or even weeks, without opening it? Do you make the effort to buy someone a birthday present, and then fail to send it in time? Do you start lots of projects but never complete them? Do you frequently say, "I'm just going to put this here, *for now*" instead of putting it away? Notice where you don't quite land the plane and start practicing a new way.

If you open a package on the kitchen counter, put the box in the recycle bin before you move on to something else. If you come home with business receipts, put them directly into your tax envelope, rather than leaving them on your desk. If you try on three shirts before work, put the two you decide against back in the closet before you leave. When we hold the resonance of completion, we are free to move forward in each moment unencumbered. As you get the hang of it, consider landing any bigger planes that are up there circling the runway; pay off that credit card, return the clothes you bought a month ago, have that birds and bees conversation with your kid, finish your taxes. Landing the plane is a radical act of self-love that keeps us in present time, and our inner and outer spaces in order.

Put Some Space Between the Notes

Cluttered souls tend to live in overcrowded conditions. The bookcase is jammed with books and framed pictures and silk plants and trinkets. The living room has too much furniture and not enough wall space. The dresser drawers are stuffed so full they are difficult to open. The refrigerator door is dripping with inspirational sayings and family pictures and exercise class schedules, all barely held together by random magnets. If you relate to any of these, you've forgotten about space.

Think of it like music. A piece of music contains notes, but what makes music beautiful is the space between the notes. Decluttering is an invitation to create space. When you release even 10 percent of the stuff in the bookcase, or in the living room, or on the fridge, or in the drawer, glorious space emerges. Making space creates room for energy to flow. This is true in your physical environment, as well as in other areas of your life. For example, do you overschedule your children? Do you run from one thing to the next? Do you talk nonstop rather than listen? Put some space between the notes. It may be unfamiliar and uncomfortable at first. You might say "Wow, it looks so empty in here" or "That drawer is only half-full, what a waste of space," or "What am I going to do with a whole hour to myself?" Stay with it until space becomes your new normal.

Separate the Thing from the Feeling

Cluttered souls tend to confuse objects with feelings. As an example, maybe you have a stuffed lion your mom gave you and you feel happy and loved in its presence. That's fine. But if you don't truly get that the love that connects you with your mom is inside you, you'll likely have *lots* of things that remind you of your mom's love. Many of them you won't even like, but you'll hear yourself say, "But I can't get rid of that. My mom gave it to me!" When we think an object holds a feeling, and we're afraid to lose the feeling, we accumulate.

Objects and feelings get confused in several ways. Sometimes we keep an object to try to hold onto an important experience. This one sounds like, "I actually hate that itchy blanket, but I can't let go of it. I got it on my trip to Peru!" Sometimes we keep an object to remind ourselves of a success in our life. This one sounds like "Oh I'm definitely keeping all those law books. They prove I made it through law school!" Sometimes we keep an object because it holds a wish. This one sounds like, "I don't like that painting but my brother gave it to me before we stopped talking and I wish we were still close." Sometimes we keep an object to remember a relationship. This one sounds like "My husband died two years ago but I'm keeping all of his clothes so it feels like he's still with me." Sometimes we keep an object because it holds the feeling of a dream we once had. This one sounds like "I have all those paintbrushes because I always wanted to be an artist."

When we forget that feelings live inside our heart, not in objects, we end up with clutter. To remedy this, trust your deeper soul knowing that you can never lose anything. Then narrow down your possessions to those that truly represent the important people and experiences in your life and honor them with a sacred place to live. If you're holding onto objects related to a dream, see if that dream is still alive in present time. If it is, wake up and take some inspired action towards it.

Your Space, Your Energy

Cluttered souls tend to live with things that aren't a match to their energy. You'll recognize these energetic misfits because they hit you with a funky vibe. You'll hear yourself say "I don't know, it just doesn't feel right" or "It's just not me." You are hereby granted permission to release that item and its energy from your space. I know it's not always easy. You might feel compelled to keep something that doesn't resonate with your energy—or you don't like, want, or need for that matter—because someone else gave it to you. Like one client said: "That fruit bowl is so not me. But I can't get rid of it because my best friend gave it to me and if she comes over she'll wonder where it is." If that's the case, consider telling yourself and the other person the truth: "Thank you, but I'm creating a clutter free and soul driven life and that fruit bowl you gave me really doesn't match my vibe." Then you'll be free to give the item back with gratitude or help it find a new home where it can be appreciated.

Sometimes we feel obliged to keep something that isn't an energetic match because it was passed down from someone else. If your grandmother's silver or your great aunt's table or your dad's fishing rod collection doesn't resonate with you, it's okay to let it go. In fact, it's more honoring to yourself and the other person to release it to someone who will truly love it and give it life.

If you find something that doesn't fit energetically, but you're not ready to part with it, see if you can transform the energy. Put it in a different area of the house and see if it feels better. Create an altar around it to change its vibration. Take something from a collection, such as one of those fishing rods, and turn it into an art piece. As always, if you're uncertain about something, leave it for the next round of decluttering. When the time is right, you'll know exactly what to do with it to honor its energy and yours.

Now if you are a person who likes to give things to others, allow *them* the freedom to say no to whatever isn't an energetic match. For example, if your son really doesn't want the train set you think he should keep for the children he might have one day, respect his wishes. If your daughter-in-law is a minimalist, find ways to connect with her that don't burden her with stuff. The your space, your energy approach frees up everyone.

Make It Soul Worthy

If someone came to your house, would they immediately know that a magnificent human being inhabits the space? This has nothing to do with the kind of dwelling you live in or the amount of money you have. It has to do with how you honor your possessions, and in the process, honor yourself. I'm constantly amazed by how people disrespect the stuff they claim is important to them. For example, are the clothes you bought with your hard-earned money scattered all over your bedroom? Is the crockpot on top of the fridge covered with cobwebs? Are your most treasured photos squashed in a broken-down box in the basement? Is the floor of your closet a filthy mess of dust and broken hangers?

Most people don't treat their stuff or the spaces that house them with reverence. To see this in action, come with me to the place I take all my clients. Yes, that's right, the cupboard underneath the kitchen sink. I know, it's scary. We know what lives in there. Here's an example from one client, who is every client.

> Tom looked at me with a smile as we went into the kitchen, saying, "Seriously, it's not that bad in there." As he opened the cupboard, I replied, "Okay great, let's have a look." We sat down on the floor, side by side, staring into the abyss. He mumbled, "Oh wow, when you look at it from down here . . . ."
>
> To me, it was the usual. Half-used spray bottles of cleaning products crammed against the pipes. Rusty aerosol cans, dried out jars of silver polish, and dirty rags stuffed in the back. A giant ball of plastic grocery bags shoved to the side. Used sponges and steel wool in front, resting in a sticky layer of gook, origin unknown.
>
> I looked at him and said, "Soul worthy? I think not." And then we laughed and pulled everything out of the cupboard. We released a bunch of nasty stuff and cleaned the cupboard thoroughly to upgrade the energy of the space. We neatly put back only what he needed in present time and, voila, the cupboard was Tom-worthy.

The fact that we've chosen something to live with us automatically makes it sacred and deserving of a place of honor. To bring the sacred into your life, you don't have to light candles and "Om" over the junk drawer. Just do your best to make every space a soul-worthy, mini-piece of art. And I mean every space: the basket of magazines by the toilet, the laundry room shelf, the inside of the refrigerator, and the workbench in the garage. Make it so everything is easy to see, easy to get to, clean, neat, and orderly. As we beautify space by space, our home becomes a soul sanctuary worthy of us and the things we love.

Come Out of Exile

As you declutter your possessions, you might come across aspects of yourself that are in exile. Very often, these forgotten aspects are of your soul nature.

For example, did you lock your creative self away in the attic with your old portfolio? Did you relegate your love of baking to the back of the cupboard with your KitchenAid mixer? Did your free spirit get trapped in a controlling relationship? Did you stop singing when the kids were born? Did you hang up your rock climbing shoes to climb the corporate ladder? If you come across an exiled part of yourself, invite it home. Break out the pastels. Make a chocolate cake from scratch. Ceremoniously release the journal from that not good for your soul relationship and start a new one. Let it rip at karaoke night. Get back on the rock. Very often, what we find in exile becomes something our soul can't live without.

Say Yes to New Life

As we declutter, things in our environment take on new life, in service to our soul intention. For example, the mini-trampoline you found in the basement becomes your go-to exercise equipment, supporting your intention to be strong, fit and full of vitality. The purple chaise lounge from the living room fits perfectly in your new she-shed, supporting your intention to start doing art again. The window seat that was previously piled high with books and papers becomes a meditation spot, supporting your intention to live in peace and calm. The bookcase that never felt right in the den is perfect for the outdoor gear in the garage, supporting your intention to get back to nature. Here's an example from a client.

> *Stephanie and I were decluttering the garage. When we got to the bottom shelf, there was a grimy old box sitting way back against the wall. I went to pull it out and it was surprisingly heavy. As I was grunting and rotating the box to slide it out, Stephanie was saying, "That is so weird, what the hell is that?" Once it was out, she laughed and said: "Oh ... I know what it is." I opened the box and lo and behold it was an old typewriter that belonged to her grandmother! Now that was an interesting coincidence, as the day before we were working in her office and had ceremoniously renamed it her "studio" to honor her soul intention to live more creatively and write a novel. She said, "Maybe we should just leave it there."*
>
> *I, of course, was not having that: "Oh no. We're gonna liberate it!"*

We took it out of the box and placed it on a stool in the garage. It sat there in all its glory. Stephanie shared some stories about her grandmother and how she was a great writer. Then she teared up, and said, "I loved my grandma. She was ahead of her time because she was able to use her gift and most women couldn't. I always felt bad about leaving my creativity behind once I had kids." I asked, "Well, how can we honor that and change the story?"

As she was thinking about it, I remarked how marvelous the typewriter was; cool in an old-school way. And then it came to her: "What if I made that the centerpiece of the shelf in my new studio? Almost like an altar with some of my special things around it. That would be awesome. It would be like she is with me, helping me write." And just like that the typewriter had found new life, born from liberating it and connecting with her grandma's spirit for support.

Soul desires inside of us also take on new life as we declutter. For example, the photographs you find in the basement remind you how much you loved horses, prompting you to volunteer at the local stable. The college transcripts you find in the office reignite your dreams of teaching and propel you to the local adult education program. The grief you find in the back of your heart becomes an impetus to serve others who are struggling with loss. Say yes to new life. Consider it magical confirmation from your soul that you're on the right track.

Let Go of Recouping

As people declutter, they invariably think it's a good idea to sell some of the things they no longer want. Nice idea of course, but it is very often the ego at the wheel, trying to recoup their losses. With a heavy dose of guilt, it will say "you spent a lot of money on that designer dress and you're not just gonna give it away!" It will insist it's still worth what you paid for it five years ago. It will demand you take it to the consignment store to get back the money you "wasted on it." It will obsess about posting the dress, and everything else, on Ebay, ignoring the fact that you don't have the interest, skills or bandwidth to do that. Rest assured you can never do enough penance to satisfy your ego mind. If you let your soul weigh in, you might find you are content to simply thank the item for its service and bid it a fond farewell. As one client said, "Thank you beautiful shirt for making me look so cute, now go forth and make someone else look cute." Now if there's something of true value you decide to sell, great. Give yourself two weeks. If you don't land the plane in that time, release it.

Summary

Physical clutter stems from the not enough of our ego mind. Freedom from clutter becomes possible when we commit to keeping only the things that support our soul intention in present time. To release physical clutter, accept where you are and stay dedicated to your freedom. Get present with your possessions and the spaces in your home to see how they feel emotionally and energetically. Sort your stuff. Use the magic of 10 percent to release what gets in the way of serving your love with the world. Land the plane. Settle into the look and feel of space. Untangle confusion about objects and feelings. Make sure your space contains your energy. Honor the things you've chosen to live with you and bring anything in exile back home. Make every space soul worthy. Celebrate new life. Delight in allowing what you no longer want or need to move on and be of service to someone else. As you clear clutter, space is created for things of your soul. This is the way of physical decluttering.

TWELVE

STAYING THE COURSE

Flowers unfold slowly and gently, bit by bit in the sunshine, and
a soul, too, must never be punished or driven, but unfolds in its
own perfect timing to reveal its true wonder and beauty.
—Eileen Caddy

As you declutter, you will find yourself engaging with life differently. Suddenly the crumpled blanket on the couch matters, and you fold it neatly in a simple and radical act of self-love. Gossiping becomes a clear energetic no, because speaking light and love feels better. A friendship that no longer feeds you is set aside for true nourishment. The tax records from 12 years ago go to the shredder because you're more loyal to present time energy than just in case fear. Your interest in consuming and accumulating wanes, supplanted by a clearer commitment to better the world with your unique gifts. Celebrate these places where you hold the resonance of your true nature.

At the same time, remain curious about where you struggle to hold the resonance. How did that mail pile up again after it felt so great to clear it last week? Why haven't you ridden your bike for a month when it made you feel strong, alive, and free? How is it that you got swept up in your friend's emotional crisis and ended up on the couch for two days, drained and exhausted? As you travel the road to freedom, your ego will invariably retake the wheel. After all, you did work late a couple days last week and were just too tired to sort the mail; and it was easier to stay home than strap on your riding gear; and your friend really needed you, didn't she? This is the ego at work, trying to keep you where you are. Even though piles on the kitchen counter and feeling out of shape and being energetically compromised are not one bit comfortable, they are familiar. And there's comfort in what's familiar, no matter how uncomfortable it is.

If you see old habits emerging, fear not. You're not backsliding. Your ego mind is just challenging the new resonance. Your only job is to accept what is and keep observing carefully. Not judging, observing. Be gentle with yourself. Go slowly. Trust that when you're ready to hold a new resonance, you will. You can't yell at a flower to bloom after all. But you can give it some water and a little more sunlight. Here are some strategies that will help.

Something In, Something Out

From this day forward, when you bring something new into your life, be sure it's something that supports your soul intention. And when you welcome it in, let go of something in exchange. For example, if you buy a hip new shirt, release one of your old ones or something from another category of clutter, such as last month's fitness magazine, or one of the three Diet Cokes you drink every day, or the resentment you feel every time you find someone else's laundry in the dryer. Something in, something out helps us interrupt the habit of accumulating and hold the resonance of releasing.

Step Away from Other People's Clutter

Very early in the decluttering process, you will begin to fixate on everyone else's clutter. You'll judge your partner's clutter or your brother's clutter or your neighbor's clutter. You'll point your finger at them. You'll implore them to deal with their stuff. You'll convince yourself that you can't declutter unless they do. You might even try to manipulate them to get rid of things.

When you notice these behaviors, stop your ego in its tracks. Stay on your side of the street, focused wholeheartedly on your clutter only. As you do, people in your life will respond. They might get inspired to look at their stuff, or they might dig their heels in deeper. Either way, let it be okay. If someone is interested in what you're doing, by all means share what feels right—with their invitation, not unsolicited. From love, rather than the desire to change them. The resonance of a decluttered soul is one of acceptance, allowance, and trust that everyone is exactly where they should be. Hold it.

Rely on the House of Mirrors

As you declutter, you will see your ego and your soul reflected everywhere you look. For example, you'll notice people inhabiting their false selves; burying themselves in stuff, eating poisonous foods, living with dirty or broken things, inciting drama, feeling bad more than good, judging themselves, or fighting for status. You'll also notice people inhabiting their true selves; trusting their preferences, saying the right thing at the right time, honoring boundaries, expressing gratitude for what they have, exuding good vibes, minding the environment, or accepting others for who they are. Be grateful for every reflection and stay dedicated to offering a soul reflection to the world.

Share Freely

Many people have more than they need, and others are in need. As an example, if you have a storage unit, it probably houses a useful resource, like maybe a couch. Now imagine all the storage units in the world, fortresses of unshared abundance and stagnant energy. Think of all the units with perfectly good couches in them, and all the people with limited financial means who need a couch! It's staggering.

What you hold onto is potentially more valuable to someone else, so re-*mind* yourself often: "that's mine" is the ego and "what can I give?" is the soul. Become a living example that there's more than enough to go around. Share whatever resources you have: possessions, words of wisdom, money, emotional understanding, artistry, or hugs. Remember, the true value of what you have lies in sharing it. When you share, everybody wins. Notice the other person's joy when they receive something they need. Feel their gratitude that they haven't been forgotten. Appreciate the soul integrity you feel as you hold the resonance of generosity.

Gift Wisely

Going forward, consider birthdays and holidays as opportunities to gift wisely. As a gift receiver, be sure anything you ask for gets a clear **yes** to all the questions. And if you don't want more stuff, make that declaration to your family and friends—to do so, you might need to declutter your fear of asking for what you want! As a gift giver, choose soul-affirming gifts for your loved ones; such as an experience they'll never forget, money to put towards a dream, something that helps them serve their love to the world, precious time spent together, or a priceless letter about all the things you love about them.

Remember the Truth

The truth is, we're only here temporarily. Many people come to the end of their lives without taking care of their stuff, be it their house full of things, or their regret for the way they treated a family member, or their last will and testament. When we hold the loving resonance of our souls, we're inspired to take responsibility for our clutter instead of leaving the burden to someone else.

THIRTEEN

ENJOYING THE TRIP

To penetrate into the essence of all being and significance, and to release the
fragrance of that inner attainment for the guidance and benefit of others, by
expressing in the world of forms truth, love, purity, and beauty—this is the
sole game which has any intrinsic and absolute worth. All other happenings,
incidents and attainments in themselves can have no lasting importance.
—Meher Baba

Our soul is inherently free and our true nature is love. And we also travel
through life with an ego mind that orients us toward fear, lack, self-preservation, competition, and holding on. Unfortunately, for many of us, the ego has
a death grip on the wheel. We speed and swerve through life in a trance of
deficiency and discontent, oblivious to our soul nature and accumulating all
kinds of clutter along the way.

All forms of clutter reflect the same thing: a soul not being true to itself.
Decluttering is an ongoing process, because every moment is an opportunity
to choose the **scared** of the ego or the **sacred** of the soul. Even as I write this,
in a doctor's waiting room, I've been witnessing my *terrified of medical stuff*
ego and my *all is well* soul vying for the wheel. All morning I've been checking my spelling ... letting stressful thoughts pass by like clouds ... holding
space for the scared little girl on the curb ... staying grounded and in my own
energy ... being present enough to share my love with the staff and allow their
certain and confident vibes to love me back ... and saying a kind no to the front
desk person offering me a business card so as to keep my load light. (You didn't
really think I was going to end this book without calling out business card
clutter, did you?) More than a task to complete, decluttering is a way of life.

In the face of a powerful, relentless ego mind, and a culture that affirms all things ego, living from the soul can feel a bit like driving the wrong way on the highway. But knowing and living our unique and common soul nature is what sets us free. With the certainty of who we are and the knowing of what we came for in the driver's seat, life becomes a completely different trip. We find ourselves on the open road, singing along to "Enough is Enough" while our ego sits quietly in the passenger seat enjoying a bag of Cheetos.

As we follow the roadmap, thoughts, emotions, energies, ways of relating, and possessions that are not of our essence reveal themselves and begin to release. Inspired action creates space for new inner and outer experiences that are more in alignment with who we really are. We become more clear-minded and less afraid. We trust our intuition. We spend more time in the energies of acceptance, joy and gratitude. We engage responsibly and collaboratively with other people. We honor the other seen and unseen beings that share our world. We keep our inner and outer environments soul worthy and in present time. We appreciate and are satisfied with what we have. We let thoughts, emotions, experiences, and stuff come and go without holding on. We focus less on what we think we need and more on the only thing that matters; taking natural and practical action to love the world in our unique ways. This is us in our right minds, at home in our being, grounded in our true nature, unencumbered, and standing soft and strong as creative livers of soul-driven lives.

As we roll through life this way, we recognize that everyone we encounter is also a soul in a human body, with their own inherent love, freedom, and unique expression. We are all in this together, on a journey to wake up to who we are and put our love into action to benefit the world. Because we are all connected, my liberation is tied to yours, and yours to mine. So free yourself. You might just free someone else. And allow others to live freely in their true nature. It might just set you free. Most of all, enjoy the trip! Remember, it's the only one worth taking.

RESOURCES AND FURTHER READING

We are all just walking each other home.
—Ram Dass

This section honors the human beings who have helped me on my road. They each offer unique guidance for healing, transformation, and restoring the soul in our world. I've also included two soul-inspired communities from my life that can help you remember your true nature.

Mental Decluttering

Byron Katie

Loving What Is: Four Questions That Can Change your Life. Eubery Publishing, 2008

I Need Your Love – Is That True?: How To Stop Seeking Love, Approval, and Appreciation and Start Finding Them Instead. Rider, 2005

A Mind at Home With Itself. HarperCollins, 2017

www.thework.com

Andy Shaw

Creating A Bug-Free Mind: The Secret to Progress. Self-Published 2nd Edition, 2012

Using A Bug Free Mind: Manifestation Unleashed. Self-Published 2nd Edition, 2012

www.ABugFreeMind.com

Emotional Decluttering

Ron Kurtz

Body-Centered Psychotherapy: The Hakomi Method. Life Rhythm, 2007

Grace Unfolding: Psychotherapy in the Spirit of Tao-Te Ching by Greg Johanson
and Ron Kurtz. Potter/Ten Speed/Harmony/Rodale, 2011
www.hakomi.com

Jon Eisman
The Hakomi Institute of Oregon
www.meta-trainings.com

Energetic Decluttering
Francesca McCartney, Ph.D.
Body of Health: The New Science of Intuition Medicine® for Energy and Balance.
New World Library, 2005
Intuition Medicine®: The Science of Energy. Intuition Library Publishing, 2001.
(Supplemental mp3 audio downloads can be found on her website)
www.intuitionmedicine.org

James Van Praagh
Talking to Heaven: A Medium's Message of Life After Death. Compass Press, 1998
Adventures of The Soul: Journeys Through the Physical and Spiritual Dimensions.
Hay House, 2014
www.vanpraagh.com
www.jvpschoolofmysticalarts.com

Energy Healing Practitioners

John Lavack	jmagick1@me.com
Barbara Reed	Barbara@IntuitionForAnimals.com
Kathy Fitzgerald	https://kathyfitzgerald.as.me
	kathyfitz330@gmail.com

Relationship Decluttering
Leza Danly and Jeanine Mancusi
www.lucidliving.net
lucidlivinglearningportal.com

Soul Inspired Communities
<u>Omega Institute for Holistic Studies</u>
www.eomega.org

<u>Super Soul Sunday</u>
www.oprah.com

ACKNOWLEDGEMENTS

Mom: for your intuitive heart, independent spirit, and encouragement to be light

Dad: for being the dad you never had, and the man you are

Sharon: for all you are and all you do to make the world a better place

Patti: for being the best wombmate, and for all your heart contains

Bobby, Brad, Joey, Hailey, Jordan, Max, and Alix: for being family love

Mr. Peabody: for bringing the canine joy

Linda Blouin: for walking so many miles in loving presence and soul commitment

Carl Schwartz: for writing the truth on the canal bank and being a friend for the ages

Jan Casalena: for opening a portal to healing

John Casalena: for your smart brain and dedication to love

Ralph Haines: for letting love win

George Adair: for integrity taught in the original Omega classroom

Steve, Melissa, George, and Elisia Harder: for experiences that mattered

Ivy Rose McClure: for being the Roo that filled the pouch

Joel Parse: for sharing, snuggling, and trust

Nikos Kilcher: for living your rhythm

Meher Baba: for coming that day at the beach

Rob and Ingrid Cooley: for the vision and fortitude to serve families and nature

Martha Shimeall: for meeting on the trail time and time again

Tricia Daly: for the freedom of all things wild

Ian Magnus: for being the best brother a girl with no brothers could ask for

Ron Kurtz: for rebirth

David Baldwin: for the loving rewire

Jon Eisman: for holding hands on the run home

The Omega Institute: for being home and family forever

Elizabeth Lesser: for expressing in the world and traveling realms together

Carol Donahoe: for eyes bright with purpose and love

Kathy Fitzgerald: for being living permission to see beyond

Jenn Brown: for embodiment, Thursdays on the patio, and your ever-seeking heart

Glenn Black: for trusting, truth-telling, and sticking around

Robert Cole: for being the angel of history

John Bashew: for all the production adventures, real moments, and balcony time

Pema Chodron: for jogging that day

Tama Kieves: for being a generous writer and friend

Susan Ariel Rainbow Kennedy (SARK): for walking in magic

The Entities of Light: for healing

Francesca McCartney: for new roads, soul friendship, and integrity beyond measure

Michael "McMaster" McCartney: for truth, neutrality, and epic soul adventures

John Lavack: for the sanctuary of healing friendship

Warren Bellows: for always painting a new door to walk through

Libby Moore: for the love and work of freeing

Lisa Erspamer: for every bunny/money experience

Oprah Winfrey: for tea house summits, nose hugs, and moments of soul truth

Andy Shaw: for being a regular bloke with a lot of wisdom

James Van Praagh: for eagles soaring on a wing and a prayer

Deb "dancer" Jones: for rising from the ashes

Tammi Leader Fuller: for Campowerment and EVOL

Deb and Jack Cantrell: for being living proof of the power of decluttering

The Campowerment family: for fun, transformation, and laying in the dirt

The Wisdom 2.0 community: for teamwork and adding love to the world

Byron Katie: for being a kindred and knowing the way

Monica Lewinsky: for naming this book and for living gratitude

Kathleen Flaherty: for remembering what matters

Leza Danly: for release parties, snacks, and lucid loving friendship

Jeanine Mancusi: for holding the space and then stepping into it

Liz Wiltzen: for being willing to look and see

Susan Casey: for spirit adventures and your invaluable help at the beginning

Aunt Dot: for being a fave and growing every day, 90 and beyond

Chris Holiday: for being a fallen angel and rising still

Laura Beier: for leaving early to serve a bigger purpose

Bob Urich: for being a big-ass guardian

Kelly Madrone: for walking the name you chose

Mary Ann Bohrer: for sharing your gift to declutter this manuscript and give it life

Jessica Waite: for essential feedback at just the right time

Bill Gladstone and the entire Waterside team: for giving my words a place to land

Kenneth Kales: for your editing largesse, air quote decluttering, and kind way

Nana and Papa: for the lineage of courage and commitment

Grandma Elsie: for being an unseen teacher

Grandpa John: for showing up to the party

Granny Goodwitch: for knowing God, squirrels, and the power of French toast

Grandpa Max: for safety and the love of trees

Cousin Tommy: for spreading love as the dandelion

Uncle Carl: for knowing about the genie in the cigar tube

Aunt Donna: for always picking up the phone, here and there

Uncle Charlie: for being a surprise unseen helper of this book

Aunt Mary: for your free spirit

Natasha: for divining the way, epic wags, and filling in the blanks together

Wairo, Toure, the Seven Mountains, the K, MB, and my star: for bringing everyone home

All my ancestors: for walking alive in spirit, at peace, eyes to the light, hearts in the trees

All my clients: for sifting through clutter and freeing us both